Before & After SCI

James Waitzman

Book Cover Design by James Waitzman
Book Cover Rubbings by William Waitzman
First edition 2023

ISBN: 979-8-218-22983-2

Contents

Dedication

Dedicated to my unwavering Father, Mother, Sisters, Brothers, Grandmother, Brothers-in-Law, and Sister-in-Law who define unconditional love. My talented, loving service dog Lee, and the friends who had my back — you know who you are.

Acknowledgments

Thank you to my sisters, Michele and Mary Ellen, who had to endure my inept punctuation. A big thank you to my family and friends, who read the original blogs and complimented its content.

Thank you, Paul, for your candor and encouragement.
Edited by Paul Vlachos

Foreword

I had the unlikely, yet great fortune, to meet James Waitzman, when we were 14 years old. *Unlikely*, because we were so very different, he lived miles away in an area of Westchester County, New York called Yonkers and I was a city kid, residing in an apartment in The Bronx. *Great fortune*, because despite our many differences, we attended The Halsted School (our parents' idea, trust me) where we were a class of only 25. Such was the foundation of a family of friends who virtually became siblings, as everyone knew everything about everyone else. Little did I realize that this would form the foundation of a treasured friendship that has spanned decades, many miles, and has morphed over the years. Back then, weekends were spent in the company of some configuration of our tribe, as we sped off in a car known as "The Bomb". Jim and his best friend Bill (whom I dated for a half a minute, thus earning me a front-row seat in The Bomb) routinely referred to each other as "Boy." It was not unusual to hear one of them shouting "Boy!" and we all understood who was being summoned. Their friendship endures to this day, and yes, they still call each other Boy!

Jim was a wild child who came into my life in high school, and he has been in my heart ever since. We are closer today than we ever were as kids, though for several years, we lost touch, or connected via mutual friends remotely. We fully reconnected in 2009, when our class created a 30th high school reunion; our school had long since been shuttered. By then, Jim was physically unable to attend in person, so we made it a point to call him from the venue, assuring that in this way, he was there with us, connecting with everyone who attended. And it was on that night that we promised him we would come to South Carolina, where he now lived. A contingent of us traveled to Charleston, South Carolina, in June 2009, making good on our promise. Trust me, if you have ever been to Charleston in June, you would understand this to be a gesture of tremendous and unparalleled love, as the humidity and heat of the low country will blow you away in the summer. Such was our continued commitment to Jim and the love we share to this day.

When we were 24, I was busy figuring out what kind of adult I wanted to be, while living in Massachusetts and drumming in a band in Boston. I had not yet decided to fully grow up, but the idea was under some consideration. That same year, while living with his parents in Yonkers and working as a union carpenter, Jim was equally disinterested in fully entering adulthood. He happily prioritized and continued to be the outdoor enthusiast I'd always known him to be. Jim lived to engage in anything outside that involved his body, movement, athleticism, activity, and adventure.

Life changed on July 27, 1985. He woke up early that morning, during a visit to the Hamptons, and he went for a walk. By that evening, he would be supine on a gurney, and he would eventually learn that he'd broken his neck, and he was now paralyzed. Only three weeks earlier, he watched the NYC July 4th fireworks in front of the very hospital that would now save his life and where he would begin his long journey to learn how to navigate his new life, as a C-5 quadriplegic young man. Jim would later say that this was the day he also broke the hearts of his family and his friends. His first helicopter ride (to the hospital) introduced him to emotional and physical pain that no 24-year-old is prepared to know.

Indeed, Jim's life would change, and many would say, irreparably. I would say that is quite a misleading conclusion, and far from the path I've watched Jim travel. The Waitzman family rallied beside Jim. We should all be so fortunate as to have the kind of parents and siblings that Jim had, as every one of his clan made it their personal mission to travel this path alongside him. He was never alone, while I am certain, in his mind, he was as frightened and frustrated as any young man could be, having his treasured independence lost, and his ability to directly negotiate the world changed forever. Perhaps if it had not been for that summer day in 1985, you would not have met the man I am introducing you to now.

My friend Jim has traveled a long way. He was not an *eloquent* teenager. Sometimes brash, at other times hysterically funny and often good natured. Yet, there was never a time when I would have told you, "he has a way with words, he should be a writer." Therein lies the gift of an unplanned life, and the kinds of catastrophic events that can alter our path forever, yet which set a course that provides for far more than could have been imagined. Jim has found his voice in these writings. I savor them as I embrace his tender ability to reminisce about well-spent and misspent youthful moments. We can only imagine the process of regaining one's life after a traumatic injury. Jim teaches us how it can be done and done well. And, he reminds us that there are many ways to embrace this gift of life, if you choose to look carefully.

Before SCI, we meet a young man, who shares his passion for life, his great love of family and friends, and youthful experiences that will bring you back to your own childhood adventures and emergence into adulthood. After SCI, well, we are taken on a sensitive path that begins with a lesson in "if" and "when", as Jim reminds us that *if* generally expresses a wish, and *when* expresses a resolve. Jim takes us through the many if's and when's that have intersected his recovery and his life after SCI. While this pivotal moment changed the course of Jim's life in many ways that we can only imagine and fear, I must say that, on so many levels, the man I know today exudes a depth and sensitivity rarely acquired, yet greatly needed in the world today. Permit me to introduce you to my dear friend, James Waitzman.

Through the stories you are about to read, you will see what I mean. Those of us with able bodies walk through our lives, never noticing many things we take for granted. How smooth is the sidewalk you're walking on? Will a small fissure send you flying out of control? When I enter a restaurant, my attention centers on the menu. Never the many issues that are potential barriers to simply getting inside the door. When your body is no longer under your control, you live a more vulnerable existence. The only thing you can control, your body, is out of your control. But if you are Jim, you come to rely upon sense, perceptions, sensitivities, and appreciations that you'd never have otherwise considered. As you read the stories that follow in the pages ahead, Jim shares a perspective few really recognize or will ever know, though they should. When I walk through the world with Jim, my awareness becomes enhanced by his view.

While some may believe that stories which center on remembrances of a life once lived differently are akin to "living in the past," I invite you to pause and look deeper, with Jim. His words paint quite a different landscape. Rather than settle into a perspective of regret, Jim revisits moments that remind us to laugh, to cry, to smile at irony, and to recognize our humanity. In the absence of having a body he may control at will, Jim shares his heart, and adeptly curates the tender moments he's lived and now discusses, within an assortment of stories that remind you that, as long as you are breathing, and you can think and perceive - as long as you can consider what is possible, not impossible - you are very much alive. And you have a great deal to offer. Tomorrow is not guaranteed, but Jim has spent nearly four decades embracing life from a perspective few know personally, and all may benefit from experiencing, with him. Our friendship, and his unique ability to bring me into his world, have enriched me forever.

I am honored to have been asked to introduce you to my dear friend and adopted sibling, James Waitzman. I have had the great privilege of learning from him and with him. I believe you will find his stories touch your heart, make you laugh, make you reminisce about your own life's missteps and tender moments. I believe you hold in your hands a wonderful treasure and I trust you will agree. It's all about the moments and how you choose to embrace them.

Ellen G Stein, Ph.D.
San Diego, California

Introduction

"It's great to be here. It's great to be anywhere."
—Keith Richards

When I awake each morning, along with the countless souls who have dodged the grim reaper, I give thanks. The genesis of my life journey as a paralyzed man occurred at Shinnecock Bay. Immediately, I knew I had suffered some sort of neurological injury. In those precious seconds, face down in the water, my countdown began. Each second that ticked by drew me closer to the inevitable — complete loss of precious air, having no option but to succumb. My God, drowning, this is how I am going to die. A second passed. My buddy turned me over and I drew a breath of sweet air. That was my second breath of life — birth, being my first. Joe cradled me as I told him I can't move a thing.

Chapter 1

My First Helicopter Ride

When I traveled down the East River Drive, as a boy, I always got excited as we approached the small helipad at 60th street, tucked in next the 59th Street Bridge which served as a shuttle to the airport. I surely didn't know which airport, I just assumed that it must be to JFK, since LaGuardia Airport was so close. If I was fortunate, a copter would take off or land just as my mom's car drove by. Our destination was usually Orchard Street, where mom did some shopping and bought my basketball shoes. After shopping, we made our regular stop at Katz's deli for pastrami sandwiches, and Dr. Brown's soda. Cream was my favorite. The meat was hand sliced, thicker than most, and loaded high on rye bread. On my first visit, I saw that a lot of the sandwich makers had finger cuts, and bandages wrapping their wounds. It was unappetizing; I got over it. On our return trip home, I did my recon for the copters. Their maneuverability captivated me and I hoped to fly in one. Probably not, that's just for executives and the rich, wanting to get to the airport and avoid the city traffic. Still, it was another fascination that a trip to the city offered.

"Whoa, we just got you in by an inch or two, the police officer said, what are you, six foot four? Did you play basketball?" I replied, yes, I played since I was a boy, through high school. The officer asked me if I was any good. I responded I had a few good games. He then told me he was starting up the engine, and we will be in the city soon. I was in a New York City Police helicopter. The year was 1985. It was July 27th, after dusk. They strapped me to a gurney, with my head and neck immobilized, held securely with dangling weights. I had broken my neck. The copter rose and sped away.

We did not go to the 60th Street helipad that I loved passing by as a boy. It was closer to land on the 34th Street helipad on the East River. The flight was quick, and the officers were constantly checking on me. To this day, I do not know why a New York City Police helicopter came out to the Hamptons to retrieve me. I am most grateful. The only other option was an ambulance ride down the Long Island Expressway, which would have taken a considerably longer time, and possibly caused more damage to my injured spinal cord.

I was anxious. My life was no longer in my control. I was in the hands of strangers, caring strangers. In this sickening scenario, I had been granted my boyhood wish. They transferred me from the helicopter on 34th Street to a waiting ambulance, then to Bellevue Hospital, where most trauma patients go. Just three weeks earlier, I was with my buddy Dan, parked on 1st Avenue, in front of Bellevue, watching the July 4th fireworks display on the East River. We arrived. They informed me that my family was waiting close by, which comforted me.

The day had started out peacefully. I woke up early and went for a walk. It was my third visit out to the Hamptons from Yonkers, where I lived with my parents. I was twenty-four, working as a carpenter, mostly in and around White Plains, NY. Selfishly, I was more interested in having fun, rather than becoming a man and finding my own place to live, like most of my peers. I loved sports: golf, basketball, ice hockey and softball. Other activities included hiking, rock climbing, camping, and boating. In a split second, that life ended. A new life began, with vast amounts of emotional and physical pain. Being the selfish person I was, all I thought about was how this injury was going to affect my life. Everyone else was secondary. That day, I not only broke my neck, I broke the hearts of my family and friends.

Chapter 2

My Bronx River Valley

The waterfall was flowing with its usual winter serenity - crack. Dee vanished. His hands and head quickly emerged from the freezing water. His cry for help resonated between the apartment buildings and the parkway embankment. Fear was on his face, his eyes were in a circular panic. There was not much for him to grab onto. Will and I scoured the river embankment, seeking a branch. The place seemed swept clean, as if a landscape company had been there before our visit along the western shore of the Bronx River.

Dee was eleven, Will and I were both twelve. We had traveled along the river, played near the waterfalls and wood bridges. I caught my first fish there, walked the nearby Harlem Division - Metro - North rail tracks for years. Dee stabilized himself on the broken ice edge and positioned his body northward against the flow of the river. Will was a Cub Scout and suggested that we lay on the ice, then grab on to each other and pull him out. We shied away from getting that close to where Dee had cracked a hole. A man and two girls were skating near us. We started waving and screaming to get their attention, which worked.

A 6-foot tall, 200 pound man and the girls that were with him skated our way. How the hell is this big guy not going to fall through the ice too? Luckily, he was skating from thicker ice, approaching Dee from the eastern shore. He got about two feet from the hole in the ice and pulled Dee out of the water, cradled him and skated back to the eastern shore, where we all piled into his Volkswagen bus. We arrived at Dee's house in less than ten minutes. The fire was blazing in the family room hearth as usual. It never went out — I mean, never. I'd place a hefty bet with anyone who claimed there would not be a fire glowing in the middle of a summer afternoon. Who needs a shredder?

All the four boys in the family had a pair of green, high rubber boots with yellow laces and had their socks inside of a plastic bread bag that was folded over the top of the boot. Quite clever of their mom. Their feet may have been cold, but they never got wet. I heard Jake harshly ask about his other boot once they settled everything. Dee had used his brother's pair that day. He did not know that the river took it. Thank God for the big skating angel, Will and I did not have the skill set for a rescue. They presented Will with an award from his Cub Scout pack. Much like our present-day participation trophies, everyone's a winner. That gentleman was brave to even attempt such a bold move — he was surely a hero that winter day.

I grew up with both brothers, practically living at their home. A favorite activity in our linear slice of the Bronx River Valley was putting coins onto the railroad tracks and retrieving them.

The steel wheels and rail compressed the shapes, creating treasures. Mostly we sacrificed pennies but, occasionally, we would use a nickel or dime. To gain access to the tracks, we walked a few blocks north of the station. We slid down the small hill and jumped off the retaining wall at

Bronx River Parkway - 1989

the curve, giving us just enough hiding space from the authorities. We could hear the train coming close to the station and we always called out, "third rail" reminding each other to watch their step when we scrambled back to the safety afforded by the wall. It was dangerous, but it was a hell of a lot of fun. Not all of our coins were found. The trap rock that was packed between the wood ties and rails concealed some. We examined our little treasures, swapped out sizes, shapes, and thoroughly enjoyed the coolness of how this hunk of machinery transformed our coins. Here, I enjoyed my first foray into the industrial arts.

Living on the northeastern ridge in Yonkers afforded us easy access to the village of Tuckahoe, which was about a mile from our neighborhood. The official claim is that there are seven hills in Yonkers. I disagree — there are more that are not included in the count. Yonkers officials wanted to equate the seven hills of Yonkers with the seven hills of Rome. Romanticized chamber-of-commerce babble. That's just my take on it.

The New York Central Railroad increased its ridership when developers built up our hill in the late 1800s. In 1917, they constructed our home on the top, flat part of the hill. On any weekday morning, you can see people walking down the hill, using the enormous stairs to catch a train north, or to the city. We would use these stairs as part of our route to Tuckahoe; for our haircuts, Carvel ice cream, Roma's pizza, and visits to the five-and-ten cent store. I loved the five-and-ten cent, where I bought rubber spiders, Spaulding balls, balsa-wood gliders, and rolls of caps for my cowboy guns. There were bins of goodies in every aisle. We were driven there by our parents if a bike needed tires or something heavier had to be taken to a merchant in the village. For a few years, I rode a cherry-red Columbia Twosome around the neighborhood. Most times I soloed the two person bike. I loved maneuvering that long rig around corners.

Our neighborhood played a crucial role in the delivery of fresh water during the gap between the completion of the old and new Croton Aqueduct. Many people referred to Parkview Avenue at the base of our hill as "the pipeline." Well, it actually was a supplemental fresh water source when the New Croton Aqueduct was being built. A pipe from the source of the Bronx and Byram River's emanated at a point near the Kensico Dam. The buried cast-iron pipe ran along the Bronx River Parkway, through Hartsdale, passing under Ardsley Road to Scarsdale Road, then to Parkview Avenue, which runs the length of the old neighborhood. In 1884, they fed the water from the fifteen-mile long pipeline into the Williamsbridge Reservoir in the Bronx until 1925. Generations have passed, the authorities decommissioned the pipeline. Parkview Avenue is still a narrow, semi-straight roadway atop a cast-iron pipe that once served New York City. Following in the next thirty years, they put the New Croton Aqueduct into service, along with the Catskill Aqueduct, which was constructed across the western valley of our hill and the Delaware Aqueduct lies deep under our ridge. I wonder if the name "pipeline" is still uttered?

Beginning in 1972, one of the sweetest activities Westchester County authorities put together was closing a section of the Bronx River Parkway for cycling. They did this early morning on Sundays. The southern starting point was Garth Road in Scarsdale, ending at the Westchester County Center at Route 119. For me to get to Garth Road, I had to ride up Parkview Avenue to Scarsdale Road, which had no sidewalks and was narrow, to boot. It was over a mile after negotiating the last section of Colonial Parkway, which most in my neighborhood called "Snake Hill." Once you arrived at Garth Road, you hung a left, peddled north on the BRP, and it immersed you in a beautifully forested section of the parkway, gliding down a slight incline. It was magical! The easy glide was short-lived. The steepest hill came up fast, and my legs had to be stroking hard in order to reach the flat road. The remainder of the ride was an easy cruise.

I would usually do the route solo, early in the morning, reaching the Westchester County Center in under forty-five minutes. It's hard to believe that back then, cruising on my green Schwinn ten-speed that I bought from a neighborhood guy, that I never had the common sense to fill my water bottle. It was a quick trip. I watered up when I got home. Life seems strange if we forget to grab a prepackaged bottle of water or fill a reusable vessel. I try to use the latter. Biking on the parkway was a highly enjoyable, seasonal Sunday activity. I have an especially fond memory of my dad sitting in his chair on the concrete patio in the backyard, reading the Sunday paper as I returned home.

That pleasant memory comes to me often — it is one of many — how simple and wonderful my childhood was.

Chapter 3

Outlook

In the old neighborhood, Outlook Avenue — strangely named "avenue," for a street a mere two blocks long — was the place to find your friends and shoot the breeze. Most drifted there to get into a pickup game or hang with a mix of the older guys on the north end — five and six years older than me. Those were my brother Doug's group, numbering at ten or more, depending on who migrated over to this hub and what day it was. Weekday's after 4pm, half were Catholic school kids on homework lock-down. The only school days benefit that some of us in our family received and enjoyed was a 2pm, Wednesday dismissal from public school for our Catholic, religious instructions at St. Eugene's. A peculiar practice, seemingly not under the law of separation of church and state, but I was not complaining. Get screamed at by a nun or a public school teacher? Easy — the wailing old nuns in their black and white garb never intimidated me. They would certainly not whack a ruler on the hands of a public school kid. One public school student from my junior high punched a priest. That was an oddity. For reasons unknown, they granted us dignity. My two older sisters had the full parochial experience. They were lifers.

Before venturing the one block east, to Outlook, the five-year-old me enjoyed the usual things of a boy my age. I would not classify myself as a sadist, but I enjoyed cooking the carpenter ants that infiltrated the aging maples with my dad's large magnifying glass. I loved suiting up into my hand-me-down yellow, then red rain gear in a downpour and create dams where the road dipped into a lower concrete slab at the head of our driveway. Another favorite activity was ripping up the tar globs at the road's edge. It eased my aggression. Our yard had symmetrical, mature plantings which gave me plenty of places to hide my whittled sticks, which I used to start small fires.

My Boyhood Pride and Joy

I would play behind the pines, azaleas, and rhododendrons and when nature called, I peed in the front, side and backyard without detection. My mom still tells the stories of my fires on the side of the house. Trust me, they were small, just big enough to torch a few captured Axis troops — I took no prisoners. They were melted; their remaining glow was stomped upon and covered with a layer of sand that was left over from the construction of the house. I treasured my pocket knives. They were proud possessions. I had two that had once belonged to my grandfather and one larger one with a Champion spark plug logo on its side, given to me by my father from a promo item at his auto parts job. We always had cool swag — jackets with Purolator filter patches on the back, as well as Pennzoil, Quaker State, and STP stickers. Brother Doug commandeered a set of goggles by ANCO windshield wipers that had battery powered wipers that moved back and forth. I'm sure that they were a hit at college.

I didn't make my sports debut on Outlook until I honed my skills with baseball and football tosses in our front yard. We played most of our basketball in my backyard, where my older brother and dad set up a backboard. Dad brought home some black, threaded pipe that mounted the goal three feet out from the house, so when completing a layup, you didn't crash into the garage. We had good games in the backyard, very comfortable for three-on-three games. I got my chops from my dad and brother Doug on how to throw and catch a football and baseball. Doug would throw a football ahead of me and had to wait to see if I caught it as I emerged from the side yard. My dad always gave me a look when I would catch a baseball without both hands on the glove. I said dad, look at your glove, it's from the 1930s, you need to have two hands to receive the ball. He replied, "what if you're in the outfield and you catch the ball with just your glove hand up and your opponent is going to tag up on your fly catch? He has at least one step on you." Dad was absolutely, fundamentally correct. These days you'll never see someone catching an outfield fly with their non-catching hand right next to their glove. It is a shame the proper way of catching a fly ball is gone. It's all about the showmanship.

To show your coolness, we fourth graders would swear up a bunch against each other. If you weren't swearing and spitting, especially when playing ball with your friends, you were some kind of peculiar. When not playing sports on the avenue, me and my punk friends watched the older guys play, and searched the curbs for firecrackers or unopened pistachios. Why did they dye those small bags of pistachios red — aesthetics, I guess? Back then, we all thought that there were two kinds that grew on different trees.

In fourth-grade, the so-called genius of the neighborhood challenged me to a chop fight. At my young age, I knew what a chop fight was, and I certainly would not get into one with a tenth-grade guy. I declined, and he found a willing victim to word battle against each other's mothers. Potch was a nasty, greasy-haired guy, an occasional upper Outlook hang around — sports were not his thing. When we hit ninth grade, he became useful to our gang when we needed someone to buy us beer. He always helped himself to a six-pack from our case.

Mark was a mild-mannered, pleasant fella to me and my brother Doug, one year his junior. He made his walk to the top of the street from an adjacent neighborhood to get into a street football or basketball pickup game, just like all the older guys. Mark was a weekend hang around, being a parochial school guy. One Saturday became quite different from the norm. It started with name calling, escalated by the big bully on the block. There were occasional pushing and fights, always one-on-one. Big bully started in on Mark, an easy target, and quickly they were down on the street. I never saw a fight on the avenue that was a stand-up, punch throwing type of brawl. Big bully landed a few soft, body blows here and there, which seemed like kidding around. Big bully escalated the encounter with a few heavy hits, and it was on. The fight became intense, quickly moving closer to the property line of the big bully's house, where his cranky father always sat inside the screened-in porch. I don't know if his father heard the screams when Mark was absorbing punches, defending himself the best way he knew how. Doug and I were within

14

ten feet — two of the few rooting for Mark to throw a punch, but he wasn't a fighter and that would not happen. That next scream that was heard resulted from Mark biting on the big bully's hand, right between the thumb and the index finger, where that thin webbing of skin resides. Wow, our guy had drawn some serious blood with his chompers. When the big bully jumped up and ran home, his hand was a bloody mess and Mark had blood on his face. Chalk one up for the good guy. There was no need for Mark to run home, he was the victor. I was happy for him. Unfortunately, he was persona non grata on the upper block — ostracized for showing up big bully.

I had my squabbles with a family on Outlook that had two wise ass brothers, separated in age like my brother Doug and myself. Guys in fourth and fifth-grade weren't putting up their fists and swinging either. Whomever got the other guy in an inescapable headlock was the victor. Tapping out of a fight required an audible, "UNCLE." I clamped down on Ray's neck twice, in front of his driveway, and he got me once, in front of mine. There was no home base advantage. Fighting was just a small activity on the avenue.

There were three basketball hoops, two on the north end and one on the south, in front of Dee and Jake's house. We lovingly named that hoop the ball breaker. The backboard bracing that was attached to a swamp maple tree had its hoop directly over the edge of the curb. When someone scored, there was an extremely good chance of the ball coming straight down, hitting the edge of the curb and popping up, cracking you in the nuts. Get hit once, you'll fear that location when trying to box out your opponent.

During the summer, especially on the fourth of July, one family always had fireworks. They would light off whole bricks, lots of firecracker packs didn't ignite, giving us a field day the following morning. We stripped them down with our pocket knives and started flash fires by the curbside. Jake occasionally got a hold of a few ash cans, and cherry bombs, which he used to blow up decayed trees at the edge of the schoolyard. Being up north, where fireworks are illegal, we treasured each boom.

Beginning in fourth grade, we investigated the enormous Catskill Aqueduct that ran the length of the ridge, west of ours. The massive, underground pipes emanated from the Kensico Dam, a New York City watershed receiving and distribution dam from the upstate Catskill and Delaware systems. I knew of it from visiting my aunt and uncle's house, where it ran parallel to their backyard. Hanging out there, was entering into P.S. 32 territory, which could be seen from the rooftop of our home school, P.S. 28. It was a walk down our ridge, crossing Central Avenue, then a hike up the path, past the posted, "NYC Watershed, Do Not Enter" sign. Once atop the hill, there was a big pump house. We sometimes saw work trucks there, but were never fortunate to catch a view inside. When we hiked up there, we were always outnumbered and chased by our public school rivals.

After the original, Old Croton Aqueduct (OCA) was operational, NYC constructed three more aqueducts, all relying on pumps to deliver water downstate. There were too many valleys running per-pendicular to the southern flow toward the holding reservoirs to rely on gravity. The gravity fed, 41 mile long, OCA was a marvel, dropping thirteen inches in elevation per mile. Engineering was put into use from the aqueduct knowledge of the Roman Empire. I delighted in knowing that the decommissioned, hand dug, hand masonry constructed tunnel flowed underneath the parking lot and ball field of my high school. My dad often drove us over, then alongside the Kensico Dam, to see the giant aerators that shot skyward until the early 1970s.

Our younger group was heavily into street hockey. When we reached junior high school, we challenged two of the four elementary, feeder schools to street hockey games and cleaned up. We had a great goaltender and many accurate shooters. I relished in keeping my goaltender's line of sight clear. We also cleaned up in intramural games in the junior high school gym. Outlook was filled with sports memories. We played football, basketball, and countless hours of street hockey. I loved to chalk up Jake and Dee's blacktop driveway with the Philadelphia Flyers logo, with the encircled "SPECTRUM" included. No one minded, being that they were diehard Rangers fans. My friends knew their team stunk. We used dead tennis balls to keep bounces to a minimum and from reaching the storm drain.

Plastic pucks stung and nobody was running home after school to put on shin guards. Jake would emerge from his family room, where he heated his plastic blade, fashioning it with a serious, illegal curve. When one of us would send a blazer at the stockade fence, it would immediately prompt Mrs. R. to the side door — no more hard shots at the fence boys. Okay, sure thing, Mrs. R. She was a saint, putting up with our crap. Dee and Jake's family room couch and table were my home away from home. My mom worked the graveyard shift at an orphanage on the Hastings-on-Hudson border with Yonkers. She was the overnight infirmary nurse for quite a few years. My mother needed her sleep, so I hung out on the avenue. By afternoon, my backyard basketball court was open for a shoot around and games.

I am thankful for my abundant childhood at the top of our hill, and slightly beyond.

Chapter 4

Horsehide

In our neighborhood, our "Field of Dreams" was a rock hard, pebble strewn infield with a decent mixed species grass outfield. There we played five on five, right field fungo games. The batter would hit the non-pitched ball between first and second base or try for a homer. Defensively, there was a first and second baseman and three outfielders. There were plays on the runner from an outfield throw and also to second base. On a rare occasion, the second baseman would run to third for a play on the runner.

I usually played first base and one of my responsibilities was to hustle to home plate and defend it from a runner coming from second or third. The right field fence, which was on top of a four-foot berm, was 200 feet from home plate. If you cleared it over the fence, that was a round tripper. We would love to stand on that berm and scale the chain-link fence to pull down a potential home run. My favorite glove in elementary school was a black, gold trimmed Al Oliver model — one of many that I bought and traded for with my paper route earnings. We all took turns jumping the fence to retrieve the ball. Those games were lively, and we played until dinner was ready, usually at six. The Hillcrest Lakers was a local sports club that used "our" field a few times a week, beginning in June. Me and my friends hated being kicked off the field by their managers. One day, we would not budge. We continued with our five-on-five fungo game until Yonkers' finest roared into the parking lot. One of the Little League managers pointed me out as the ringleader, which pivoted the two cops in my direction. Yes, I was one of the defiant loudmouths. Being nearly six feet tall in seventh grade, I stood out, which was not to my advantage in this situation. One cop told me to come to the rear of the backstop and read a particular line on a yellow piece of plywood that listed the schoolyard rules. Something about yielding or stopping play for organized clubs. I was certainly aware of this rule.

Now what? He told me to wait for him at the squad car. I knew enough at age twelve that you were to do as told. As I was walking to the car, I had a powerful urge to make a run for it. The first hill was thirty feet away. From there I would sprint the forty yards to the next hill, which was our steep sleigh riding hill, which was overgrown in June. Then, I would cut through yards, zig-zagging my last leg to home. I knew I could lose them on the second hill — but I respected authority that day. Not one of my friends on the ball field that afternoon would have ratted me out. I was in my first cop car, caged in, doors sealed. Now, I had to endure the blah, blah, blah of my high-crime on the three blocks ride to home. We arrived, the two cops knocked on the front door and when opened, I could see them talking to my brother Bill, who was indifferent to them.

They left the property and hopped back into the car. The one riding shotgun spun my way and screamed, "get your ass to Police Head-quarters this evening with a parent." I kept my mouth shut as they released me from the squad car. Dad was not a happy camper. We drove over the western hills of the "Terrace City" without saying a word. We entered the building, and they directed me to speak to the desk sergeant. He was expecting me. He read some formalities and barked at me, "go home!" My dad finally blew a gasket when we reached the Saw Mill River. He gave me the, "when I was a kid" lecture as I kept my pie hole sealed. He did not say it, but I think he would have preferred that I made a run for it.

When I was in my early teens, the older kids in the neighborhood would gather in the summer afternoon at our field. There would be enough players for two full teams. Some older kids measured the entire field and spray painted the footage on plywood boards. They nailed a 200 foot sign to a utility pole in right, center field was 320 feet, attached to a chain linked fence at the path, and they marked the left field stick ball wall at 275. Pitching was 3/4 speed. Nobody wanted to have some ace striking out the side every inning — we wanted the ball in play. I got to play in a few games at second base. When there was an overflow of the older kids and I had no chance to get in the game, I would umpire at first base. Those couple of summers were so cool, how through word of mouth, so many talented ball players from the neighborhood came together. One made it to the Texas Ranger's Minor League team in Asheville, NC.

I had dual loyalty. My dad grew up a Chicago Cubs fan, and I followed them, enjoying their rivalry with the Mets. I also followed the Yankees. In 1973, when most of us were twelve and thirteen, we formed a Yankee club at Barry's house. We would meet for our own version of spring training as soon as the winter mud had dried.

Pitcher and catcher tosses, infield practice, and hitting in his large backyard. We also planned group game trips into the Bronx.

The subway cars lurched laterally. The 4 train from Woodlawn Station to the Yankee Stadium stop at 161st Street was mostly straight. Still, it was a hazard to remember. The five to six of us from our club liked to ride outside, between the cars, holding onto the door latch or a hand grip that was bolted on either side of the train doors. We planted our Chuck Taylor high-tops firmly on the curved steel end of the train. There was about a six-inch gap between the cars, which was a concern. Having a firm grip was important. If you couldn't handle a surprise, lateral jolt — the only thing that could save you were three pieces of chain, horizontally attached to one vertical chain on either side of the train. If you fell over that, you would be a grease spot on the street.

Riding on the 4 train to the stadium during the 1972 and '73 seasons became fun once we got off the number 20 bus that lumbered down Central Avenue from our neighborhood in Yonkers. The bus trip was less than seven miles, but it stopped so frequently that you felt like jumping out and running alongside. Woodlawn station was the end of the line in the north Bronx, just a stone's throw below Woodlawn Cemetery, where many famous and infamous of NYC made their last stop. The cemetery is quite impressive; name a celebrated person from the 19th and 20th century and it's a good possibility they were interred in either a mausoleum or a plot. They constructed cemeteries back then like parkland. Loved ones would make a day out of it when visiting their departed. My father and I drove around the enormous grounds a few times, and found many of the rich, famous, and notorious. It was quite the history lesson.

After a five-mile train ride to the stadium, which left you off in center field, it was time to purchase a ticket. In those bad old days of 1972 and 1973, when CBS owned the Yankees, seats were easy to purchase, even on opening day. The Steinbrenner Group, with George as the primary stakeholder, began acquiring top players immediately. Walking home one winter afternoon, my friend Jake popped his head out of his bedroom window screaming, "Steinbrenner just got us Catfish Hunter!" It was 1974, a big get for a hefty sum. By now, the free agency doors were kicked wide open, thanks to the brave move that Curt Flood, the Cardinal's centerfielder, who refused to be traded on the Cardinal's terms in 1969. Players who challenged MLB's reserve clause followed Flood's initial, righteous action. There have been signing wars ever since. At that moment, I knew the Yankees would soon be a team to be reckoned with. Three years later, they landed Reggie Jackson. That became the genesis of a new Yankee era.

It was the seventies, and the subways were nasty. Graffiti covered the cars and most of the windows, leaving you no option but to stick your head out of the double doors to read the stop location that was written on each I-beam. Straining to hear the location announcement was futile. You knew the stadium stop because of the volume of riders who headed to the doors. We figured strength in numbers, but sometimes there were just two of us when we headed out to Shea Stadium during the two years that Yankee Stadium was being renovated and the Mets shared their ballpark. Trips out to Shea required a transfer to the 7 train. We all had the fear of getting mugged. I kept alert, never locking eyes with another rider.

The old stadium had wooden seats that we would slam up and down during rallies. After the third inning, we would make our way down from the cheap seats and grease the palm of an usher to sit in a box seat. They knew who was showing up by the third. The ushers wore red suits with matching hats. They had an imitation sheepskin mitt that they would use to wipe down the seats. Lord knows who laundered those cootie pads last. It was well worth forking up a buck to sit in any empty box seat throughout the horseshoe of the stadium.

I loved the steady noise level of the fans and vendors when I walked back under the seats to buy a hotdog. Decades of dark material were ground into the pores of the concrete. "The House that Ruth Built" was showing its age, but its history could never be erased. In deep center, there were three monuments in the playing field at the flagpole. These huge, granite and marble tribute stones with plaques honoring Lou Gehrig, Babe Ruth and Miller Huggins hindered many players trying to retrieve a ball in play 461 feet from home plate. I was fortunate to attend games at the original stadium. I still recall my first walk out from the refreshment corridor and seeing the expanse of flawless green grass.

Our Field of Dreams is still there, not much improved from my heyday. After receiving Lee, my service dog in the spring of 1992, I had to show my boy where I attended school and played ball. It was the only public place that I let him off his leash to roam the entire field. I would follow him up to the old, "green monster" stick ball wall and then make my way back to the parking lot. Periodically peeking at Lee and seeing him peek back at me, until I arrived at the infield, and I had to get serious with him. First call, normal tone — second call louder tone with inflection — got him sprinting back to the heel side, and I gave my command for him to leg up onto my

24

thigh for the leash hook up. Before returning home, I would visit for a moment at the corner of the backstop, waiting for my turn at bat.

Chapter 5

Tennis, Anyone?

A t age 15, me and my neighborhood buds were introduced to the gentile sport of tennis. Not the traditional, full-court tennis that was played on clay at the neighborhood Colonial Heights Tennis Club, next to our elementary school. This was a hybrid, one-third sized, elevated structure called platform tennis. Rules and scoring were mostly the same, except for allowing play off of the honeycombed, twelve foot high wire walls. The strung, long-handled racket was substituted with a short-handled paddle, which had fifty, three-eighth inch holes drilled through it, allowing for lower resistance on the swing. The solid rubber ball was heavier than a tennis ball and enveloped in felt. We would regularly wear a ball of its felt after a few sets.

Since this was a sport developed for tennis to be played in the winter months, they painted the decking of the platform with coarse, sand-like material that wore down, not only the ball, but your shoes too. The hinged, lowered boards folded up to shovel and brush the snow off the deck. We rarely groomed the deck, most our court time was in decent weather. We all loved it. The game was fast, with long volleys, and best of all, it was free.

We sought out the few scattered platforms in lower Westchester County. The first court we played at was not a club. It was at Sarah Lawrence College in Yonkers, NY, nestled among the pine trees near the modern section of dorms. We played there during the day, even though lights were available. Our second location was in Bronxville, which had multiple platforms that we used legally, courtesy of Dave's mom's boyfriend, who lived in the town. We played those courts mostly at night. Leewood Country Club in Eastchester was our third option — one of Babe Ruth's old clubs. There, the platforms were far away from the golf course and clubhouse. No one ever challenged our member status. Enter, and act like you belong, and you can blend most anywhere.

As for being gentile, tennis lacks the physical, direct contact, but it got fiercely competitive and heated when we played. Our styles mirrored those of the stars of our era — the considerably obnoxious John McEnroe and Jimmy Connors. Playing so close to one another at the net was intense. We contended for every point, like every other sport we played. When I watched tennis on television, which was primarily the Grand Slams, my dad would kid me, saying "tennis anyone." I would love to hear him say it, knowing that tennis was a lot harder and intense than he thought.

Dad was brought up playing baseball and football with leather helmets, minus the face mask. Years later, in my wheelchair, dad and I enjoyed playing tennis together. When we moved to Carolina, we first lived in a sprawling apartment complex that had a tennis court in the center. I had taken up tennis with a group of wheelchair users at St. Andrews playground in Charleston. I went for the camaraderie, and to learn how to crush a few from my chair.

Back then, my chair could accommodate my joystick on either side — when I played, I reversed the armrests, and drove with my non-dominate, left hand. Physical therapy volunteers wrapped an ace bandage around my hand, and racket — tight, affording me an unobstructed swing at a bounced ball my way. I couldn't track down balls hit to me very well, but I sure enjoyed hitting one over the net, in the sweet spot of the racket.

Playing at the court, outside my bedroom window at the apartment, was a beautiful bonding experience for me and dad. He would feed me a bounced ball, which I hit towards all areas of the far court. We would go through many baskets full of balls, collect them, and do it over for hours. I enjoyed those times with dad, immensely. We came full circle from our days playing football and baseball in the front yard. Now, it was me asking dad, "tennis, anyone?"

Chapter 6

'77

A lot went down in '77. The .44 caliber killer was out there somewhere. NYC was in a heightened state, most were anxious. Foolishly, my evening habits mimicked the victims that spring and summer. I was making out in cars, keeping it local — in Pelham and Glen Island, in New Rochelle. In April, four "parkers," in two locations, fell victim, but our raging teenage hormones took precedence over the potential danger. My suburban cocoon was altered only by the occasional cruise to the city to do all-nighters, visit the Empire, the Towers, or a concert. Ironically, officers arrested Berkowitz, aka "Son of Sam," on August 11th, at his apartment, a half mile north of my high school.

I first met my lifelong friend Bill, in the early fall of '76, while shooting early morning hoops in the school gym. We introduced ourselves and he told me he was from Pelham. In the Bronx? "No, it's in Westchester, east of Mount Vernon, south of New Rochelle." The only Pelham I knew was from the movie, *"The Taking of Pelham One-Two-Three."* Bill and I became fast friends. We took the first leg of the bus ride home together. I usually walked the remaining mile home, blowing off the transfer. Bill continued into Bronxville, then transferred onward to New Rochelle, where his final trek was a two-mile walk home. We did this bus drudgery together until basketball season started for me. At year's end, Bill invited me to a house party in Pelham. Upon arrival, at the parentless home, I could hear Zep's, *"Houses of the Holy,"* thumping and was enveloped in a packed house of gals and guys.

That was where I first saw her, wearing a floral-patterned black blouse. She was talking on the kitchen phone as she repetitively tossed an orange upward and impaled it with a knife. I was smitten. We didn't speak that night. I was way too shy, and she was out of my league. I had an ace up my sleeve and didn't even know it. She was not interested in any of the guys in town. They had all been friends since elementary school and I'm sure she looked upon them more like brothers. Sanford was a fellow basketball teammate from my town who began dating her, also cheating and making disparaging remarks about her in my presence. That was when she began skipping Thursday night swimming class at the YWCA and hung with me. Our favorite make-out spot was Glen Island at night. I told her she was way overdue in confronting Sandy and getting the breakup done.

He had played another asshole move when he pulled a blade on a town local who was walking with his gal through the woods near her house. Sandy was over confident and fortunate that Nick granted him mercy. That small town, spring news traveled like wildfire. His behavior embarrassed her, but she was still hesitant to break up with him. It was not my job; it was hers. I agreed to one term, have Sandy come to me. He did, unexpectedly, accompanied by Ricky, as I was relaxing on a couch in Ralph's room — the town party house. Ricky

32

raced up the stairs, giving me a ten second heads-up. I kept my ass planted on the ratty third floor couch as Sandy paced back and forth on the worn oak floor, repeating, "that's my woman." After he concluded his pathetic diatribe, I reminded him of his activities and told him it was best to leave. I stood, giving him a chance to swing or attempt to kick me with his raised Frye boots. He chose the smart exit. I was the second other guy from Yonkers, an outsider with no history in the town. In time, "we" seriously began.

My studies at high school were in summer recess. I was invited to Bill's folks' place in Bridgton, Maine. He was scheduled to work the summer as a camp counselor across from their home on Moose Pond. We took turns driving his Fleetwood on a route that was seared into Bill's melon. "The bomb" was showing her age, but she still had more luxury than most, and her giddy-up was still giving. I was entering virgin territory for a week of exploring western Maine before he was due to report.

We had strict instructions from his mother to camp on the property until she and Dr. Clifford arrived in two days. The no-see-ums had their way with us that first night. We had a decent tent, but it was no match for those little buggers. Bill would not go through another night of misery and it thrilled me to hear him say, "Jim, we're breaking in." All it took was a bit of pressure on the bottom of the sliding glass door and we were styling. What a relief to spend the night in a comfortable, bug-free environment. He cooked up some mac and cheese and we were golden.

The next morning, we hauled ass back down to the tent and waited for his folks at our makeshift campsite. We heard Bill's mom calling us from the house. We exchanged pleasantries, then Mrs. C. got right down to the nitty gritty. "Boys, in the future, you need to cover your bases better." Oh, shit, we were busted, but how? "You would have gotten away with it, except for the bits of macaroni in the garbage disposal, and the radio was tuned to a rock and roll station." She was pissed, but nice about it. I was relieved that we didn't get a good yelling at.

Bill and I packed a lot of activity into my first visit. The cold, pristine waters of Moose Pond were fabulous. It was quite large, mostly long. If this is what they called a pond, I can only imagine the enormity of a lake. On a late afternoon canoe trip from across the pond, Bill kept telling me to be on the lookout for a loon. Back then, I couldn't tell the difference between a loon and a turkey. Halfway back to the dock, we heard the haunting call of a loon. It was fabulous! We didn't see it initially, but it was spotted and quickly submerged. When the magnificent loon finally surfaced, it was half a football field away. Quite an experience, a fabulous memory.

Pleasant Mountain was down the road a bit, so we climbed it and, just as we reached the summit, two fighter jets flew over us. That was a treat. The closest town, other than Bridgton, was North Conway, NH. We headed there for groceries, which included the mandatory purchase of the famous, snappy, red hot dogs at Shaw's. There was always a lot of activity at this gateway to the Presidential Mountain Range. We picked up a hitchhiker en route, who jumped right into conversation. "Hey, are you guys gangstas?" Gangsters, why would you say that? "Well, you got this big Cadillac with New York plates and me and my friends were talking." Bill had fun with him. "Yeah, we're gangsters." He ripped that retort in a nanosecond. We were both six-foot four-inch, sixteen-year-old longhairs that hardly fit the gangster profile. The only item I possessed with any affinity to a gangster was a black banded, wide rimmed fedora I swiped from my brother. We circulated this Al Capone replica amongst us back in Pelham, where it currently was. Our next encounter with the locals was two guys who wanted to show us their car. "Fastest in the county!" After hearing that line multiple times, our curiosity grew, and we took them up on their offer. Dusk was upon us, but it wasn't too far out of town. The "fastest car in the county" was a half-tarped Dodge Charger, up on blocks. Jeez, what a waste, just two bullshitters.

They invited us in for a cold one, and why not for the trouble alone? After the pop, and witnessing inept, aggressive commands toward his dog, I felt a bad vibe. Bill sensed it too and gave me the eye. We quickly left. There would be no *"Deliverance"* sequel. If things went south, hopefully, we could have held our own. We had no weapons — it would have been messy if they did. Nobody wants to be fertilizer in the backyard. We were young and dumb, but we had a sliver of sense that night. As Dr. Clifford would sometimes say, "The blind leading the blind." At that age, he was spot on. That week went by too quickly. Bill drove me to the bus station in Portland, where I caught a Greyhound to NYC and began my misadventure home on the subway.

By summer's end, my first serious relationship was nearing four months and its future was heading toward an obstacle. She was bound for boarding school west of Philly. It wasn't unexpected. I knew that there was an expiration date. I was determined to keep us going, despite my limited resources. My bud Larry went above and beyond, setting me up with a loaner Ford Fairlane wagon. Right before I hit the highway, Bill ran out of his folk's house with the down comforter from his bed. Now, those were great friends and I'm blessed to still have them in my life.

It was a Friday afternoon, the last week of September, and I knew most of the route by memory from road tripping my older brother to Villanova University. The Fairlane wagon only had AM radio, and I was bombarded with the hit song, *"You Light Up My Life."* Leaving NYC on the George Washington Bridge, down the Jersey Turnpike and on the home stretch into PA, the majors saturated the airwaves. After numerous plays, I let it all hang out and was scream-singing that pop tune with tears running down my cheeks.

I figured, once I got in the general area, I would ask around for the directions to her school. I started seeing peculiar looking license plates that didn't have the standard, embossed numbers, and letters. Uh-oh, where the hell am I? I got close enough to a car and saw that I was in Delaware. I overshot the school by ten miles. With the help of a friendly Sunoco gas attendant, I arrived before dark. I asked around and found her quickly. The trusty green wagon was my sleeping quarters for two nights on campus and provided reliable transportation around the area with my gal and her new classmates. We caught a showing of Rocky, which I thought was cool, being that we were in the Philly area. I ate and washed up at Mickey D's.

The ride home was emotionally draining, not knowing what our future held. How that Fairlane got me home on less than a full tank of gas still puzzles me. We were on and off for the good part of five years, with an uninterrupted year together, when she accepted a local corporate internship while on a hiatus from college. I drove her back off to college at LaGuardia Airport. Leaving that gate was rough. I returned her father's car to an empty house, where so many memories were made. It was heart-wrenching. I never felt lonelier than at that moment. There was more of us, encompassing too many spans of time, then the inevitable end. Early on, I knew, and I'm sure she knew too, we had no future together. I experienced love — its beauty and pain. Finally, I moved on and dated other gals. She had a place in my heart for years.

Maine - 1984

I returned to Bridgton three more times. North Conway and Mt. Washington were always on the to-do list. Golfing with mosquitos made for quick rounds, and that thrill of the Alpine Slide at Attitash Mountain was welcoming. Bill's folks were always gracious hosts. I enjoyed lobsters, authentic clam bakes and their company. I know how much they cherished their slice of heaven on Moose Pond. They are gone, but remembered. God bless them.

Chapter 7

Henry G and Me

In the old house, we had a mail slot beneath the bottom side light at the front door. My routine was to sit on the slate floor and sort through the letters and magazines. I received little mail, but on a late summer morning there was one letter with a return address from my school. It was addressed to my parents. What could this be about, the start date, tuition? I couldn't contain my curiosity.

I tore into that envelope and quickly discovered that I was persona non grata for my senior year at the small private school I had been attending in northwest Yonkers. It was concise. I was not being invited back for academic reasons. Damn, it's late August! Yes, I was a poor student but, in fairness, I believe I should have been given ample warning. Geometry sunk me, as most math subjects did. An opportunity after junior year to bolster my GPA by retaking the class would have been nice. There wasn't any counseling offered by the staff or administration. Wouldn't my underachievement warrant an educator's call to action? Dropping this news on me two weeks before school began was a sucker punch. Their time frame was cunning, with no opportunity for me to plead my case. I was one of four students who received the letter and none of us returned. This school prided itself on full college admittance. Their ads in the Yonkers paper touted the bogus claim of 100% college admission.

As a freshman, sitting on a second-floor windowsill overlooking the parking lot, I witnessed how privilege works. A group of seniors turned an English teacher's Honda Civic on its side, righted it, then turned it on its driver's side for good measure. Not one of those students received punishment for their actions. I'll assume that a check was cut, and everything was golden. The headmaster had a selective pattern of conveniently looking the other way. He had a Dickensian name and a sordid reputation. He had been employed at the school for quite some time, eventually taking over the headmaster position when the beloved previous headmistress had retired.

Hearing stories from others who preceded my time did not shine a favorable light on this man. Discipline and retribution took precedence over education. A buddy of mine was attending a wedding in the late 1980s and, during introductions with others at the table, he was asked what high school he attended. He replied, "A small school in Yonkers, you probably never heard of it." "My cousin lives in Yonkers and attended this school, which he named. Is it the same school?" My friend was taken aback. He knew the cousin, as did I. This fellow told my friend that the headmaster was an embezzler. The school closed its doors in 1983 and was sold soon after. Attendance was dwindling, even when I was there.

No one knew of the alleged nefarious activity of our stealthy headmaster. When the story was told to me, I took it with a grain of salt. Years later, I heard this same story firsthand from the daughter of a past board member. This second corroboration heightened my interest. Contact via Facebook and through subsequent calls with a fellow basketball teammate was confirmation. He conveyed his knowledge of the school's "relocated" money, as well as an attempted tuition shakedown by the headmaster and his minion. In my book, three unrelated sources telling the identical crime is ironclad. Mister high-and-mighty turned out to be a thief. The board removed and replaced him. That thief should have experienced time, but white collars rarely do.

One week after my late summer surprise, I enrolled at Roosevelt High School. I just wanted to get the hell out of high school. Sounded easy enough, but I lost interest and blew off my last three months. Working a job from 4 to 11 after classes added to my departure. Back then, by rule, you had to wait one month after the school year to take the GED. I drove down to De Witt Clinton High School in the Bronx for the exam. A few weeks later, sitting on that same slate floor, I ripped open my New York State Education Department letter and rapidly scanned my results of the five subjects. To pass, you had to score 70% on all. I succeeded and was proud of it. I didn't want to go through life regretting that I didn't complete high school. That GED became useful when my life changed, and I replaced my hammer with a mouse.

Regrettably, I wasted my folk's hard-earned money. I did not apply myself. Having fun was more important. There was no subject that interested me. I should have flunked out in public school from the get go, or made the smart decision and enrolled in the trade school. Our town had a fine one, a mile south. There is a silver lining here

— I met many friends that I still keep in touch with. Positive, caring, loving friends.

Chapter 8

The Jockeys & The Colonel

G rease, lots of grease. The thickness of it, the stink. Ducts, filters, hoods and fans were magnets of its nastiness. It was a toss-up, what smell was more unpleasant, the grease or the chemicals we used. My baptism into this world of grease was at a diner close to home, where we had to work around chefs and cooks engaged in their 24/7 dance. My best bud Larry joined me once and, at night's end, I knew he was done. If there was money to be made, we were on it, but this was too repulsive to him. On the next job, I stepped into the position of primary driver for East Coast Fire Prevention at age nineteen. None of the other guys in the crew had a driver's license.

We loaded the van for bear with powerful smelling chemicals that hit you hard upon entering. The lead man of the crew was Mercer, who I picked up at his apartment off East 3rd Street in Mount Vernon. I was familiar with the area. My dad worked at Globe Motorists Supply Company, down the street. We would then collect three other workers in the area. There were a few occasions when we had no-shows or delays, waiting for one of the crew to get his ass out of bed. When working for our high-end client, it required a 3am collection of the guys.

We headed down to the city for my first experience at the 21 Club. The regulars referred to the place simply as "21." I rolled in with the van and crew after 4am. Mercer jumped out and gave a loud whistle, alerting the night man on the upper floor. Numerous jockey statues lined the railing and eyeballed us as we unloaded our equipment. It was a peculiar feeling in the early morning of a quiet Manhattan. The shiny brass doors were unlocked and as I turned right, an eclectic sight was revealed to me. I was in the Bar Room, which was filled with toy models of aircraft, cars, trains, and a bunch of other memorabilia, all suspended from the ceiling. I later learned that most were gifted from famous patrons. It was an impressive sight. I didn't have the time to linger and take it all in. Mercer got a kick out of my reaction. He had been with the company for a long time, it was all old hat for him.

Our job was to eradicate the grease. We headed to the kitchen at the back of the house. It was rectangular and smaller than I expected. They converted the building into a restaurant from a previous five story townhouse. The exhaust duct from the kitchen needed to be scraped clean. It was a narrow opening which called for the smallest man in the crew to be lowered into the abyss from the roof. He sat in a bosun's chair and scraped for an hour. When he was in that duct, a strict, no aerosol policy went into effect. The rest of us had plenty to do.

The disassembled stainless-steel filters made their way into a chemical bath at the far sinks to soak for an hour while we got busy scraping inside the hoods. Next, we polished the hoods and re-installed the filters. When everything was up to Mercer's standards, I squared up and adhered our bright orange label on the side of the hood, signifying that the team and I had completed a proper cleaning and inspection. Mercer dated and signed it. We packed up and drove back to Mount Vernon. I returned to this iconic establishment two more times, where I took in more of the atmosphere. Like most bars and restaurants, you wouldn't want to see the view with the house lights switched to high.

We had two small restaurant clients in Brewster, NY that required only the boss and me. The main money maker for this company were the ten Kentucky Fried Chicken franchises we cleaned and certified in Brooklyn. I was fortunate to have Mercer as my navigator. Brooklyn was virgin territory for me, and he knew where every job site was. When on a Colonel run, I would pick the fellas up at 10pm and we would work until dawn. Each night, we would knock off two franchises. This job got old after four months, for obvious reasons. Brighter days were ahead.

Chapter 9

My First Career

I worked the second shift at a Shell service station during senior year. That was a road to nowhere. My first aim after high school was to get a decent job. I floundered from station to station, never achieving a skill other than oil and tire changes. Then I enrolled in a welding class. I liked it and continued onto advanced welding. My grandfather was a welder at the Brooklyn Navy Yard. I was following in his trade, which gave me a sense of pride. The process fascinated me, but I was getting ill from the fumes and the eventual demands if I ever landed a job. Heights for me end at thirty feet. I was going nowhere fast.

My sister and godmother, Michele, worked in one of the largest IBM buildings in Westchester County. Her gregarious, loving personality had people gravitating towards her. She and her coworkers constantly saw a carpentry outfit that was working in this vast office complex. They called him, "Tony Movable Partition." She approached Tony and asked if he would consider taking me on as a go-fer and if I caught on, would he teach me the carpentry trade? He agreed. I met Carl, Tony's partner, at the loading dock of 1133 Westchester Avenue. As a boy, I made two display shelves and a large rabbit cage. I could handle a hammer, saw and ruler. That was the extent of my skills.

The walls at this building were called Vaughn Wall. This reusable sectional system of tongue-and-groove drywall panels was very efficient. The building was built in 1969, and Tony was the carpentry foreman. He was a second-generation Sicilian, raised in Red Hook, Brooklyn. Carl was from Yonkers and coincidentally attended the same private high school as me. Tony was an exceptional teacher. He was a no-nonsense guy, but there was time for fun. The food that we ate on contract jobs, which were mostly at night, was delicious. These men liked good food. I loved the atmosphere and was making decent money. After working for their company for a year and a half, Tony asked if I intended to stay on and continue to learn the trade. I said, "yes, most definitely."

That is when he sprung the good news on me. "I'm happy to hear that, Jim. I spoke with the head of Carpenter's Local 53 in White Plains, and I want you to meet with him after lunch." This was fantastic news! I took my drive over to the union hall to meet Mr. James Nicholson. Local 53 was the biggest and most powerful in Westchester County. White Plains, being the county seat, along with many corporate headquarters, had most of the newer buildings rising in the 1980s. There was a lot of work out there. I nervously climbed the steep set of stairs, nodded to a group of guys playing cards, and made my way to his corner office. I introduced myself to this imposing gentleman. He bellowed out in an Irish accent, "so you'd like to be a union carpenter, would you?" "Yes sir," I replied. My chances of being accepted as a union carpenter were in my favor versus someone off the street being I was currently working as a carpenter and was being sponsored by my bosses at Tri-State Interiors.

Having a year and a half of experience under my belt, Mr. Nicholson asked me what year of carpentry school would be appropriate for him to place me in? I knew I was beyond first year knowledge, and I would not be a punk and say third year. I was honest and told him I believe entering the union and attending carpentry school as a second-year man would be a good fit. He replied, "that's the right answer." I was relieved and thrilled. He said to me, "you know you have to complete four years to become a journeyman?" I replied, "Yes, sir, I am aware of that." They held school in a massive building about twenty miles north of my parents' house. I attended year-round with a two-month break in the summer. Every Tuesday was a three-hour combination of classroom learning and hands-on skill lessons. I met some great guys at the carpentry center. I completed the second and third year when my life came to an abrupt halt.

My spinal cord injury in July 1985 ended my carpentry career. I never got the chance to enter my fourth and final year of school. My local had quite a few brothers. I attended meetings regularly and enjoyed the camaraderie. We packed the hall at year's end, with over three hundred members settling up their dues and enjoying a Christmas party. Everyone who didn't know each other's names shook hands and said, "hey brother." I was very active in my local, playing basketball and softball. Our basketball team was mediocre, but our softball team was stellar. We had beautiful uniforms — blue and yellow, home and away threads. My position was first base, which I earned at a chilly spring try-out. I had a sweet round tripper on my first at bat. I loved playing and representing my local.

Our season highlight was a lower New York State championship in Beacon, NY, against a bunch of other locals. It was a single elimination all-day affair. We won four straight games. Our home field was down the street from a job site I was working at after I moved on to a new contractor. Tony and Carl had given me my start, but I grew tired of working with the two of them without my buddy, Steve. He moved on to a contractor that renovated all the Citibanks in Westchester County and parts of the Bronx. When Tony and Carl employed me, I would venture to say that I worked in nearly every IBM building in Westchester County. I enjoyed plying my trade, experiencing the many unique buildings and meeting new people. It was an exciting atmosphere to be in as a young man. Beautiful women were everywhere.

Now, I was earning good money and had full medical insurance, which afforded me an opportunity to buy stuff. The first of my dream three was a motorcycle. I had that baby for a mere nine months and put eighteen thousand miles on her. After work, I cruised throughout upper Westchester County's winding hills and valleys. Sometimes I would park at Purchase College, lay down in a field, and watch planes coming and going from the airport. I wished I had someone to share those after-work cruises with. My ride was cut short when a car crossed in front of me in a hit-and-run accident. My bike impacted with the back right quarter panel of the asshole's car, wedging my left calf and footrest together. I sustained blunt force trauma to my calf, one inch above my riding boots. My bike was laying in the middle of Central Avenue, which is a three-lane road that leads into New York City. I was attempting to drag my Yamaha 750 from the street and cars were honking at me. The NYC metro area can be tough, but c'mon. A young woman and man jumped out of their vehicle and helped me drag my bike, which weighed 470 pounds, to the curbside. I asked them if they would stay and look after my bike. They did. Then I hobbled an eighth mile up to the nearest store to call on the payphone to my friends. It was January, and I had my bike in my folk's garage with the insurance taken off for four months. I was just going to take her out to meet my new girlfriend at a local bar a few miles from home. You know what they say — most accidents happen close to home.

The police showed up as my friends drove off with my injured cycle. A fella came over to me and the officers, and told us he saw everything, chased the car to the Bronx line, trying to get a license plate number. Cool guy. The police drove me to the hospital to have my leg looked after. The doctor sewed twenty internal and twenty external stitches. One police officer asked for my license and insurance at the hospital for paperwork needs. I had to fess up. I had no current insurance. He said that he understood. He had a bike himself and, like most of us, he took his insurance off during the winter months. I was happy that he was cool and did not cite me. After getting medically fixed, I exited the hospital and ran into my friend Jay, one of my riding buddies. He said that he was visiting a family friend in the hospital. I told him what went down, and he was floored. I asked him if he would drive me to the bar to meet up with my girlfriend. He did and stayed for a few drinks.

Two days later, we brought my damaged bike to the dealer, where I had bought her. The mechanic asked me if my bike was insured. "Nope." Its frame and shaft drive were beyond repair. The bike was too new to even find donor parts. Repair costs exceeded the price of a new one. The owner cut me a $500 check for the motor, which was pristine. I had her wrapped in a beautifully bent, chrome pipe with highway pegs. I walked the two blocks to the bank and made my last payments. That was the end of my motorcycle days. It was short, but it was a hell of a lot of fun! Trucks were now in my future. Months later, convinced that I was done with riding, I handed Jay my black Bell helmet. That beauty of a bike took me to the outer reaches of Long Island, up to the Shawangunk Mountains, west of New Paltz and various places in between. I drove her in the sun, rain, and cold. As uncomfortable as the weather could sometimes be, riding on my bike was always exhilarating.

Chapter 10

Ice

It was Saturday morning at 6am, and it was cold! I stepped out of the locker room, made my way to the double doors, and saw the ice for the first time. I've been on figure skates once — today, I'm double socked into a vintage pair of hockey skates, and I am not in my element. Athletics have always been part of my life, and I held my own with the neighborhood guys — this was a completely unfamiliar environment. We played plenty of street hockey, but ice hockey, especially the obvious skating skills needed, was different, very different. My 13-year-old self hopped onto the ice, trying my best to emulate the pros that I watched on our grainy basement TV set. They would swagger out of their runway from the locker room and do their quick hop onto the ice, receiving the roar from the fans.

My hop did not fare well — down I went, hard enough to spew a few f-bombs. There was no turning back. I made the commitment, and I was going to see it through. A month before my grand entrance, my mom called me into the kitchen. She was talking with our neighbor and said, "how would you like to join the ice hockey league over at Murray's rink?" Like most choices that I made in my adolescence, I said "sure", without giving it a second thought. Our neighbor had the vintage skates in her lap. I thanked her and off I went to the sports store, where I bought the gear that was required. My skates were not sharpened adequately, which made skating extremely difficult. I made it through that initial practice. My first order of business after that debacle was to go back to the sports store and buy a decent pair of skates. I made sure I was properly prepared for the next Saturday. Coach blew the whistle and gathered us in a circle around him. It was time to hand out our jerseys — sweaters, to be traditionally correct. I was given number 22, a white Chicago Blackhawks replica.

From that practice forward, I became a rink rat. Every Saturday, I would wake up at 4:30, suit up, then either jump in the car with my dad, or do the off-week carpool with my buddy down the street and his dad. Practice and instruction were usually two hours, beginning at 6am with a scrimmage for an hour against the other team in the league, who wore red Hawks jerseys. When we finished at 9am, Mark and I would ride home, eat, watch TV, then met up again for a walk back to our little Mecca. It was two miles, but well worth it. We would skate the afternoon away, most times skating back-to-back sessions.

Murray's was an open-sided rink with a steel, rounded roof. They enclosed the locker room and pro shop. The outside opposite end was open — the perfect structure for great ice. Cold air wafted in, keeping the ice hard and when the Zamboni finished its cleaning, that ice glistened. Each week, with no absence, we would spend our day at the rink. Our favorite exercise was a sprint from goal line to goal line, grinding to a hard stop to see who could flare up the most ice. We were showoffs. I upgraded to a sweet pair of Bauer skates, which eased the skin damage to my heels. As the season went on, our skating skills improved and meshed with our street hockey skills. Mark and I continued to skate throughout the summer, up at the twin indoor rinks, which were twenty miles north of our homes. By then, another fella in the neighborhood played ice hockey, so now we had another adult who could get us to the ice.

The place was a ghost town during the summer. I approached the general manager and asked him what the rate was to rent the rink for an hour. At 14, I was already 6 foot-four, so I'm guessing he thought I was of age. "Sixty bucks per hour, and I'll let it run over a bit." I told everyone who was in our league and others that we had a rink with ice time. I can't recall exactly how many rentals I put together, at least a half dozen. Sometimes we had two goaltenders, other times we were short of two full teams. In one session, we were without a second goaltender.

I was permitted to borrow Coach Hank's goalie gear. Whoa, never again. That was way too difficult, especially blocking and catching slap shots. After that experience, I had a greater understanding and respect for goaltenders. As was customary, I collected the cash, which always varied, depending on how many showed up at the rental sessions. Once, when I was short, the manager said, "don't worry, you'll get me next time." There was no next time. The enclosed twin rinks folded. Too bad, it was a whole lotta fun.

The new second season had about ten additional players. The organization, the Yonkers Hockey Association, now had two full lines on two teams. This year we wore Islander jerseys. My team wore the home white with the other squad donning the away blues. Coach Hank assigned me number 4. Bobby Orr's number! I nearly pissed myself. If that wasn't cool enough, the coach placed the blue and orange captain's "C" into my hand. He had recognized my hard work from the previous year and rewarded me. Coach then directed me to pick two alternate captains who would wear the "A." Without thinking it through, I picked two of our best players. Big mistake. Why did I pass over Mark? He was gung-ho, a motivator, and a good player. I messed up, big time. I knew right then that I hurt his feelings. The entire morning I felt like crap, but there was no taking it back. I cemented it. Mark asked me why on the drive home. I had nothing for him, only an apology. What he deserved was more, much more. He was the better fit, but those words did not cross my lips. We put that day in our rear view. At least I did.

We played most of our games against each other, with a few visiting teams coming to our house. The most exciting game of the season was going down to the Bronx to play in an outdoor rink parallel to the train that stopped at Yankee Stadium, three blocks south. We were familiar with the 4 train that had a center field stop. Having my dad drive Mark and me past Yankee stadium at 5:30 in the morning, then up Jerome Avenue to the outdoor rink was boss! In our neighborhood, if something was boss, it could not get any cooler. When we arrived at the rink, there was a light dusting of snow on the ice and no Zamboni to clean it. The home team broke out the shovels and both teams cleared the snow to make the rink usable. We couldn't suit up both teams to travel down for the game, so the coach picked an All-Star squad. I started first line, left defense, Mark, left wing. We thought, what do these city kids know about hockey? They knew a hell of a lot more than we did. We got our asses kicked. No one likes to lose, but the experience smoothed off the frustration of a whooping.

The YHA had a high school league. Coach Hank was also the coach of the Sacred Heart Leafs. After junior league, I had transitioned from public school to private school. Each team in the league, which was composed of one Catholic high school, four public high schools from Yonkers, and one from nearby Mount Vernon, were required to have an open tryout for two players who did not attend these schools. Back then, ice hockey was a club sport that received no school funding. We all chipped in for our practice and game ice time. Coach invited me to play for the Heart. Coach Hank led the team to the championship the previous year, when it was packed with seniors. The next season when I played with them, we were a shell of the swaggering all-stars from the previous year. My dad dropped me off at the Sacred Heart campus, which was up the street from my private school. It was at night, and we were to meet to receive our sweaters. It went in numerical order, with our goaltender receiving number 1.

When it came time to the handout of number 4, I did not wish or expect to receive it. One of the all-time greatest players that Sacred Heart ever had donned number 4 the previous few years. Paul was a 6 foot 2, 220 lb package of speed, with a blazing shot. Coach called out my name, and handed me Paul's former jersey, without the white "C", of course. I could hear disapproving groans throughout the assembled. Good God, I said to myself, let me just melt right here. I was an outsider, and these northwest Yonkers boys wanted nothing to do with me. Coach gave me their hero's jersey — the other defensemen were counting on getting it.

I did not dare decline the decision of my coach. They were not your ordinary store-bought replica jerseys. These were bona fide, minor league threads. Coach Hank had connections with the NY Leafs, which I believe was a minor league connected team of the Toronto Maple Leafs. They were not the blue and white colors of the NHL Leafs but were identical in fashion except for color, which were green and white. The numbers were a white silk, with the maple leaf logo having an "NY" cut out. These beautiful threads were heavier, the real deal. Midway through the season, the team got a sponsor and replaced the pro sweaters with Minnesota North Stars replicas, which had a hideous, yellow on green, "Alpine Label Company" vinyl, heat transfer block above my new number 12. Someone lobbied hard for my number 4. God bless them, filling Paul's stellar play was unachievable. It was not about the number; it was about not being welcomed and properly respected as a teammate.

Practice for Sacred Heart was at 6am, on Wednesday at Murray's — a grueling hour and a half with my "teammates." After practices, I stuffed my gear into my dad's WWII duffel bag, jumped in the Mercury Cougar and dad drove me to school. They provided no shower facilities at the rink, which meant that, other than a face wash at school, I stunk on Wednesdays. I was second line, left defenseman, as a freshman. High school hockey was another world — faster, rivalries, rabid fans. Being checked into the chicken wire, board uppers was always a treat. Two Roosevelt High forwards checked me hard as I raced after the puck in the far corner, sending me over the boards, skates high, into the crowd at the only location without fencing. Thankfully, the fans and I avoided injury, as a skate blade can rip through flesh. That was the same double door where I unsuccessfully attempted my entry hop as a greenhorn two years prior. My play was sub-par and, after five games, they sent me down to the third line, where I sat on a lot of wood. It was a fair decision by the coach. I was not ready for prime time. I would get a shift, two or three times a period. There was not any camaraderie, the enjoyment was gone. I lingered for 3/4 of the season, then quit on the team and on myself. High school hockey was over.

Organized high school football, soccer, basketball, and baseball filled the void. I picked up hockey again for two seasons, beginning in 1982, with men's league play. I teamed up with the Valhalla boys and enjoyed it. Travel distance was 35 miles from home, across the Tappan Zee Bridge and up the west bank of the Hudson. Getting home on weeknights was always late, with 8am clock-ins at work. Jimbo and I found additional pickup, men's play in Larchmont and at the art deco gem at Rye Playland, where my two uncles played for Roosevelt High in the late 1940s.

My good friend Nina made many trips to the rinks with us. She had to have a high tolerance of our stink. Thankfully, our even nastier equipment bags were in the pickup bed. Jimbo and I sought out ice. I traveled with my skates, stick and pucks, in my truck's toolbox, ready to get on the ice wherever it was. The two coolest outdoor spots were a pond behind his house on the grounds of Westchester Community College, and a long, narrow pond on the grounds of the Gates of Heaven Cemetery, at the bottom of the hill from Babe Ruth's resting place. There we would sprint and pass the puck on the glistening, natural ice. Once, we skated past closing and had to search the grounds for the caretaker. The joy returned. I was once again holding my favorite brand of stick, a white Canadien, and shooting a wrister up, into the one hole.

Chapter 11

The Roc

I immediately felt the precision of the gear lever as I shifted her into drive, and I'm equally floored by the elegance of this hand-built beauty. Lordy, my skinny butt, enveloped itself in the buttery leather seat of a Rolls-Royce Silver Shadow II. I wasn't at the palm-sweating stage, but I was nervous. There was plenty of room to navigate around the primary lot at the San Roc Restaurant. I was working as a valet, along with my best bud, Larry and crew leader, Joe.

After my loop, I parked her right up front, in the honor position. The best car of the night always rested there as the owner dined and danced inside the massive night spot. This was the treat that we gave ourselves. Yes, I know, it was disrespectful, but I'm betting most would do it too. When was I ever going to be behind the wheel of a Rolls again? I'm sure if the owners knew the liberty that we occasionally took, they would have fired us on the spot. It was worth it. Larry and I worked together with the same precision of that beauty's gear shift. We did Saturday and Sunday night stints, in the fall, winter of 1980, and spring of 1981.

We parked hundreds of cars in an evening. There would be occasions when the downstairs and upstairs catering rooms were both in use, along with the downstairs dining room and bar. On those nights, we added another guy to help park and deliver those vehicles. Sometimes they came in ones and twos, other times we would get hit with ten at a time, all lined up to unload at the main entrance. There was no walking. It was a quasi-track meet, and we ran well. After the bulk of the guests were inside and enjoying themselves, they allowed us a meal that we ate quickly at a table tucked away in a corner. I couldn't tell you how many various cars we drove. Everything from a Volkswagen Bug to the Rolls.

The main dining room had cabaret acts on the weekend. They performed a mix of standards and pop tunes. The artists rotated, but the musician I remember most was a beautiful, 40-ish woman who had a sultry voice. Her set list was consistent as we heard her belt out, *"I Will Survive"* by Gloria Gaynor at the same time each night she worked. We had it down, she usually sang it at 10pm.

Standard pay was $11, which was given to us in an envelope by Mr. B in his downstairs office. The man grunted at us and pointed to our envelope. We opened it up, separated our pay stub, signed the check and he would hand us over the cash. Off we went to start our shift. We made the real money at the end of the night when the patrons would file out and wait in line for their car to be brought up to the top ramp. Joe would open the passenger door and we would exit the driver's side, hold the door open and wait for the driver to slip us a buck, sometimes two. One night, it was just Larry and me. That was rough. I tossed him the keys, and he'd map it on the chalkboard, and

I moved on to the next car. Parking and retrieving all those cars was non-stop, controlled mayhem.

At night's end, after we cleared the lot, and only the owners and their friends stayed, we lined their cars up with the heat on, pointed forward and ready to roll. Larry and I would go into the bar and say good night to everyone and let them know their vehicles were running and toasty. They would give us a few fives here and there on our way out of the bar. The last order of business was divvying up the cash. It usually came out to a little over a hundred bucks each on an average night, plus Mr. B's 11 bucks. Winter was hard, especially running on the snow and ice. I slipped and fell down a few times. It was all part of the job description. On the rare occasion, I would receive small change, not the standard buck. The best tippers, other than the owners and heavy hitters, were the young couple on a date — guaranteed two bucks. That short-lived job paid the down payment for my motorcycle.

Chapter 12

Balloons, Floats & Carlton

We took the scenic parkway route to the city from the suburbs. Cross County to the Saw Mill, then the Henry Hudson, for our last stretch into Manhattan. This is the same route that I took for my weekend job as a doorman. Cruising through the Riverdale section of the Bronx was a sweet ride, and the journey became sweeter as we crossed over the Spuyten Duyvil Bridge that afforded views of the Harlem River to the east and the Hudson River, with the magnificent Palisades on the western edge. Jay rode his Honda, Horst, a Suzuki, and my ride was a Yamaha. We exited at 79th Street and headed to the mid-50s and 8th Avenue.

We rolled our rides back to the curb, neat and perpendicular. Horst and I were watching Jay as he walked toward one of NYC's finest. "Officer, can I get you a cup of coffee?" asked Jay. "No, thanks, I'm set." Most in law enforcement would decline. "You guys headed over to the parade?" Yup, we all replied. "Don't worry about your bikes. I'm in the area." That came as a welcome relief to us. I'll go out on a limb and guess that he probably thought we were half-baked knuckleheads, out riding in the cold. My bud Jay was the most enthusiastic friend I had. He carried himself with confidence, void of pretense. Horst, well, let's just say that he was a bit too adventurous. The masses swallowed us up as we headed over to the Macy's Thanksgiving Day Parade and took in the floats and the balloons! They glided over our heads and were much more impressive than the view from the tube.

We crammed ourselves into Rockefeller Center like sardines. Peered down into the sunken, small skating rink where the gilded bronze statue of Prometheus was on watch. Tourist time for us was getting stale, so we hoofed it back to our bikes and headed crosstown to get on the East River Drive. On the way, Horst went into, shall I say, "Horst mode" and entertained all with his version of Evel Knievel. His half block long wheelies were epic. The boy had skills. It surprised me he restrained himself for so long. It was a Go Pro moment if there ever was one — unfortunately, we were living in a Super 8 world. You never knew when he was going to pop one or stand up on his pegs. Jay and I were much more reserved in our riding habits. As we meandered through the streets, we cruised by the vicinity of my doorman job at 6 West 77th and Central Park West, facing the American Museum of Natural History. The organizers laid out the parade balloons and filled them the night before in the street, directly in front of the building. It would have been cool to see, but I had my primary carpentry job on the weekdays.

My brother-in-law at the time had a friend who was the live-in superintendent of 6 West 77th. He told me that there was an opening as a doorman/porter. I figured, how hard could it be, plus more income?

Why not? On the day of my interview, I parked my bike in front of the building, rocking the full beard and leathers, which helped beat off the cold of November. The superintendent gave me the rundown on the job description. They divided the day into two 3.5-hour shifts, with an hour of lunch. After a few more questions, I shook his hand, and he hired me. "Don't forget to lose the facial hair and never, ever knock on my door unless it was an emergency. They outfitted me with the red suit, cap included. Thankfully, there were no white gloves. They gave me the crash course of my duties in the front, back and basement of the fourteen-story property. Job one, the brass clad awning posts had to be cleaned and polished every other day. Being a weekend employee, I was good at dodging that task.

Hailing cabs, opening doors, greeting residents with a smile, and collecting their packages was cake. My personal nightmare was the elevator. It was an Otis manual, and I never perfected the level stop. I was always too low or too high and was constantly making corrections. Working that car filled me with anxiety, especially having to tell the residents to please watch their step as they negotiated the four inches up or down when entering or exiting. My other duties were to collect the garbage from the back door of the residences. Their kitchens had a door to a rear landing where they would place their garbage. All residents were neat and courteous. The rear service elevator was a manual as well, where my leveling screw-ups didn't matter. I put everything that I collected into thick, plastic bags and tied tight with strong wire that I spun with a hand tool. There would be fifty bags lined up in the basement for collection day. I did not have to bring them up and out to the street. That was for the weekday crew.

On a garbage collection round, a putrid sulfur odor was coming from one residence. I thought for a moment about whether this constituted an emergency. Yeah, it could be, so I expressed the car to the lobby to alert the super. This cheerful guy complained all the way back up, saying that this better be good. I'm thinking, hell, I hope so, but what exactly would good be? It may just be a kid in his tighty-whities playing with a science kit. He used his master key to open the steel door and right away we saw the cause of the stink. Someone had left a pot of eggs on the burner. The heat nearly burned away the contents of the pot. I suppose the pot could have started a fire; we'll never know. That was the highlight of yet another mundane job that I had. It lasted three months.

Many years later, as I was relaxing in bed in the early morning, listening to Jay's volunteer college radio gig on WVKR, he played the Stones song, "Waiting on a Friend." I sensed he was reaching out, and I immediately called the station. He was on a break, which allowed us a moment to talk. He reminded me of the reflection of the Manhattan skyline that he saw on the rear of my shiny black Bell helmet on our home bound ride that glorious Thanksgiving Day. I'm fortunate to still be in touch with Jay and the remaining friends I cherish from my pre-injury life, thanks to the wonders of the oft-maligned social media platforms.

Chapter 13

Two Ridges

My love for the outdoors began at Camp Russell on Richmond Pond, a few miles west of Pittsfield, MA, where my grandparents had me for a portion of the summers of 1970 and 1971. The camp offered baseball, swimming, and target shooting, which I enjoyed, but camping out was my favorite activity.

Whenever they announced an off-grounds hike, around the pond, and overnight camp-outs, I went. Twice a week, campers and staff would sit in rustic bleachers around a bonfire, steps from my first-year cabin, where counselors would try to top each other with their scariest stories.

Camp Russell - Pittsfield, MA - 1970

They succeeded in scaring the crap out of this nine-year-old.

My next opportunity to camp was age twelve, as a boy scout with Troop 3 Crestwood, which met two blocks from home. St. John's parish house was where we gathered on Thursday evening for our scouting lessons, Johnny-on-the-Pony, and parade dress practice.

I had the honor of flag-bearer for Old Glory — where I learned to loathe wearing an external leather cup that held the butt end of the flagpole. I endured a jabbed bladder and my family jewels housed a pressure point for an hour. We met early on Saturday morning in the church parking lot for our ride

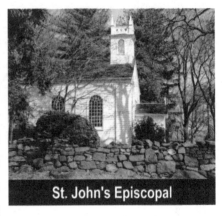

St. John's Episcopal

upstate. The main reason I joined up was for the overnights. I earned one merit badge. A primo camping location was Ward Pound Ridge Reservation, thirty miles from home. The grounds had lean-to's that provided solid shelter, and most had dual hearths. There were eight sites that I knew of, and I camped in nearly all, during my two years as a scout and into adulthood.

We also frequented Harriman State Park, on the shoreline of Lake Tiorati. Three of us from Bat Patrol pitched our pup tent amongst the wild rhododendron, to gain some shelter from the night wind. Our scoutmaster made us dig a shallow trench around the perimeter of our tent, insuring rain water from entering. It never rained on a boy scout overnight — never. We always setup the same way when tent camping. Started a roaring fire, ate nasty canned food, and talked away most of the night. Not one of us had the sense enough to leave our boots close to the fire. Slipping into those cold boots in the morning stung our dogs. On a memorable Saturday afternoon, the entire troop hiked two miles to the Bradley iron ore mine. It was up a steep hillside, through a narrow, carved out rock wall. Water filled in the abandoned mine, which gave it an eerie look. A semi submerged, wood planked walkway that hugged the rock wall brought you into a sloped, semi-dry interior, which went back into the darkness. Every time I visited the mine, which has a history of providing ore for the civil war, I got goosebumps thinking about the potential of a slip into the dark, man-made chasm. As a teenager, on cruises through the state park, I always stopped and showed newcomers.

My buds Dan and Rob were regulars at Pound Ridge, and on one occasion, sister Pat joined us. Twice a month, we would rush up on a Friday afternoon to register for the first come, first served lean-to's. We camped in all seasons, with winter visits requiring as much tarping as we could bring to enclose the open front of the structure. When the setup was complete, it was nice and toasty. The sites that I always tried to snag in winter were the hill units. Break out the sleds!

My high school friend Steve attended SUNY New Paltz, where I received my introduction to the magical Shawangunk Ridge, affectionately known as the "Gunk's," and Minnewaska State Park during his freshman year. Initially, I took the Greyhound and would stay for the weekend. Sleeping on the floor with the dust bunnies was always a nasty experience. We would catch a ride with anyone heading out west to the Gunk's. Our favorite spots were the waterfalls, where we would lie down on the flat rocks and wait for the sun to come up. My transportation came a year later with my motorcycle. We were less than amateur rock climbers, as green as it gets, and didn't dare attempt any climbs above our skill level. The safe bet was to head further west to the old Ski Minnewaska slope on US 44/NY 55, which offered a perimeter of climbable rocks that we could handle.

Climbing became a passion throughout my abbreviated motorcycle days and eventual pickup truck years. At times, we parked and walked up the incline to camp and climb. When ranger Bob finished his shift, I would ride my bike up to the top. I didn't trust the security at the lot when we headed to the top of the hill. It wasn't a huge rise, but it had its challenges. My friends with four-wheel-drive vehicles easily drove up to the campsite. Lounging on the abandoned chair lift was an oddity that I enjoyed. The views from there were sweet, but the top of the rocks, above the trees, was spectacular. Most times, we would have a full Saturday to climb, camp overnight, then hit the diner in town before our ride home. I'm sure the wait staff appreciated our reeking, smokey hair and clothing.

Riding up to New Paltz at night had its elements of danger, thanks to the poorly maintained, unlit cement ribbon of I-87. The only luxury of light was the three-mile length of the Tappan Zee Bridge. I rode smart, as most bikers do, keeping off the center, slick part of the lanes. In doing so, the occasional pothole made its acquaintance, without adequate warning for avoidance. These rides required a laser focus of the unknown hazards ahead.

On a Gunk run, I was in the good company of Jay and Horst, and yes, Horst took every opportunity to open up his Suzuki on the interstate. It was only seventy-seven miles from my front door to our planned meet up with Joe and Richie from hometown Yonkers. We settled in for a few cold ones at a college bar and needed a room to crash. I knew of a no-tell-motel at the edge of town, close to the Wallkill River. It was late, and I had the draw of registering for a room to shelter the five of us. I rang at the desk for the graveyard shift guy and paid my budget, busting thirty bucks for our rank little room.

No one got any sleep that night, only rest. Our scenic mountain cruise awaited us in the early morning.

Joe and Richie headed home as we hit the pavement toward the slope to meet Ken and Buzzy. Ken was a fellow carpenter that I met in second-year trade class. I mentioned we would be at the ski lot on Saturday morning, and they showed. No surprise there. Ken and Buzzy drove over from Buzzy's cabin near Downsville, west of the Pepacton Reservoir. Our beloved daredevil, Horst, had wandered off earlier, towards a small stream and was determined to cross it with his motorcycle. Wow, I didn't see that coming. He had it all set up with a fallen tree that he pulled from the brush. His front wheel was on, ready for the crossing.

With some coaxing, he came to his senses and backed off. At the summit, we stopped and appreciated the wonderful view of the Gunk's from all directions. The five of us enjoyed climbing various ridges that day. It was time to head back down the hill to Minnewaska State Park's Awosting Falls, where we ended our day with a hike to the top. It pleased me that the guys had an eastern Catskill experience. Ken was an avid deer hunter. I did not hunt, which limited our upstate time together. We more than made up for it, hanging out downstate, close to home. After my injury, we eventually grew apart and lost touch. We enjoyed a lot of memorable moments together, packed inside a brief time.

I have thought about my old friend many times over the years. Last spring, as I was reclining in my wheelchair, he popped into my head once more. I've tried internet searches in the past with no luck. This time, I took another approach. Reluctantly, I keyed in Ken's name and obituary and received two hits. One was a police accident report that had occurred on I-95, the other was from a funeral home. Ken beat cancer in his early twenties. Tragically, he was taken by the road. His passing was in 2016 on his spring trip north from Jacksonville. He was so close as he drove by my house. So close. RIP. Ken, front and left-center, wearing the white butcher smock.

Pig Roast at Buzzy's - Downsville, NY - 1985

Chapter 14

Windows

As I was rolling out the thick, industrial grade Austin off-white paint inside the doorway of my sister's second-floor apartment in North White Plains, I heard a knock. Come on in — the door opened, and a beautiful gal walked through the threshold. She said, "Hi, I'm Carrie." I replied, "Nice to meet you, I'm Jim." This gal didn't just walk off the street, seeing my silhouette rolling out paint in the house apartment. It was a setup by my sister Michele and her downstairs neighbor, who was Carrie's older sister.

I rested my paint stick roller against the wall and asked Carrie if she would like to talk in my sister's bedroom. I was twenty-two; she was twenty — a Yonkers gal, who lived two miles south of me in a different school district. Certainly I heard about her family through Michele. I asked her if I may have her number and called her the next day from my sister's office at IBM.

"Carrie, this is Jim, Michele's sister." I screwed that one up royally. She laughed, and I asked if she was free on Friday night for dinner. The Hilltop, a college and corporate mixed eatery, was just down the road from SUNY Purchase, which was familiar to me and close to

Carrie's home. As our conversation went on, she was talking about her old home and neighborhood, which was vacated for the new family home in Harrison two years ago. She discussed her friends screwing around and that she did not approve of it — a steady boyfriend that she had broken up with a year ago. My guy/dog mind was computing this limited, fresh data. Is she now abstaining from sex? I surely wouldn't ask this early on. Should I proceed and pursue a potential ghost ship? I made the choice to give us a try.

We started dating once a week, then gradually saw each other three to four days a week, when I visited her home from my job sites — that is, on days when I wasn't filthy. She worked for her family at their construction company in Yonkers. Occasionally, when we were in the presence of her mother, Carrie would often say, "Don't listen to my mom when she's ranting about the unions. You stay in your local and never let your credentials expire." Sound advice, she knew how things worked. Her parents didn't like dealing with the heavy equipment operators.

Carrie did some modeling out of a small agency in Manhattan. I went with her one afternoon, riding shotgun in her blinding white '63 Mercedes. I didn't care for Carrie's ride. The paint screamed at you. My ride at the time was "The Buick." Every time I asked my grandmother if I could borrow her car, she would yell back, "you mean the Buick?" Yup, the Buick. I hated the dang Buick! Had little choice. I had just purchased my bed less, Chevrolet pickup truck, ultimately finding one at a Hunt's Point salvage yard. A memorable jaunt to the Bronx, where I received a speeding ticket from one of New York's finest. That truck was an ugly beast, with big tires that served no function. I couldn't take the beast on dates. I had registered it at the

DMV with money saving commercial plates, which was a sure pull over on the passenger car only parkways. Back then, troopers and county cruisers would pull over SUVs, and vans too. If they found construction tools or building material, they would write you up.

Carrie's family home was a mile from an IBM, where I had worked on many construction jobs. We spent a lot of evenings together in the huge, sunken floor living room, as well as the front room, where we went for privacy. It was 1982 and most homes did not have a VCR and big projection screen like the one in her folk's living room. My folks had a player that consistently flashed 12:00. I did not know how to record a TV show on that machine. My skill level was limited to pushing play to start a flick. We had a "Scarface" bootleg. Movie selections at Carrie's were plentiful. I watched a lot of wonderful shows while cuddling up on the sectional couch.

On a bitterly cold January afternoon, we made our way to the New York City Aquarium at Coney Island. Driving through the streets of Brooklyn was an adventure. Mercer, who knew the borough well, always navigated my old, late night driving job with East Coast Fire Protection. I could have used his skills that day. When we finally arrived, we ran fifty feet to the warmth of the inside exhibits. The beautiful beluga whale was the star attraction. They housed it in the large tank with an inside and outside view. The moray eel that poked its head out from the holes of its home intrigued me. We ventured back out into the cold to see the remaining exhibits. Running back to the Buick, I saw the twin towers, ten miles away. That is when I had the idea to dine at Windows on the World next time I'm out on the town with Carrie.

I'm not sure, but I believe my number of visits to the World Trade Center was eight. We started going right after they opened the observation deck in 1975. I loved that you had the choice of staying inside or taking the escalator up to the outside observation deck. After a few visits, it all seemed so familiar, until I reached the glass on the 107th observation floor, and futilely tried to identify the hundreds of prominent buildings and structures.

One evening, a neighborhood buddy invited me to join him and his older brother at the towers. It was a clear evening, and we enjoyed the vast amount of lights glistening from the buildings and bridges below. We heard the announcement that the outside observation deck was now closed, and the enclosed observation floor would close in a half hour. The escalators to the outside platform stopped running, but we hadn't yet had our fill for the night. Dave and I scampered up that long, still escalator onto the closed observation deck. We were living in a different time; we pushed it to the limit and stayed past closing time. The top of the World Trade Center was all to ourselves. I was in contact with Dave recently. It's been forty years since we last saw each other as twenty-year-old's, casting our vote at the Parish Hall, across the street from St. John's Episcopal Church, two blocks north of my folk's home. It was wonderful reminiscing about our WTC night.

Come February, I made a reservation for two at the 107th floor restaurant, Windows on the World. I wasn't a credit card guy; didn't get one until I was thirty. I began saving quickly, catching extra weekend jobs. Knowing it was going to be expensive, I put together three hundred greenbacks, two covered it. I came dressed in the only sharp threads I owned — dark blue blazer, gray shirt, blue tie, dark gray slacks, black shoes, and my father's gray overcoat. Carrie wore a blue dress with a full-length blue coat and black high heels. Her long, wavy, brunette hair flowed over the front and back of her shoulders. The food was not to my liking or hers. Shrimp in jellied molds was my prominent memory. Portions were small and peculiar in the presentation. To boot, there was no distinguishable view. The clouds obstructed the magical lights. That was my last visit to the stunning towers that anchored lower Manhattan. My loving last memory was strolling out of the lobby of the north tower with Carrie on my arm towards the valet.

Carrie's mother was protective. That was her baby girl. I fully understood the mother-daughter dynamic. I believe I sunk myself when I sent Carrie a spring bouquet. She loved it and told me it was her first. I believed her, but it puzzled me; who hadn't yet received flowers at twenty years of age? My obstacle was her mom, who began to passive aggressively call the shots. For some time, she sensed I was getting serious, and she was correct. I was thinking long-term relationship. I regret not opening up more with Carrie about a future together. We may have gone further.

Chapter 15

Montauk Point & Smith Point

"What the hell are you doing here? I told you all last night that this campsite was full, and I can't even believe that your trucks are on the damn beach!" That was my Saturday wake up call from the park ranger. He was dressed to the nines, including that impressive hat. It shocked me to be woken up in that fashion. There were eight of us morons scattered about the trucks and campfire. The previous night, we tried to get in the parking lot, but as mentioned earlier, the ranger told us they were full. We had traveled a long way and had to come up with a plan. We proceeded down the road and waited for the ranger to close and lock the gates. When we saw it was clear, we made our move and went around the gates and down to the rock-strewn beach.

We were about one quarter of a mile from the Montauk Lighthouse. My truck bed was completely full of pre-cut, ready-to-burn firewood, along with a dirt bike. I was camping with the Valhalla boys. These guys were mostly in-house movers at an IBM building where

I worked for a contractor. We became fast friends, and I eventually joined a men's hockey league with them. We also participated in men's softball together. They were a group of good guys, and I enjoyed them. My best buddy Jimbo rode that dirt bike up and down the beach for the good part of the night. It was so windy that once he got a hundred feet away from the campsite, you could no longer hear the loud exhaust. I arranged my trusty tent off the back tailgate, which gave shelter to the four of us. The rest of the group slept in their SUV. Camping was one of my favorite activities; this was the ultimate, to be so close to the famous lighthouse. We were fortunate to be let off with a stern warning. We apologized, but he didn't want to hear it. That was completely understandable. We had to find a new place to camp.

Mark was driving his Bronco with his girlfriend, who lived in Suffolk County. Being a resident, gave us entrance into Smith Point County Park. It was sixty miles down the road and they had beach camping for vehicles. We hauled ass down to the park, and luckily were issued a permit to enter and exit the beach at will.

Smith Point - Suffolk CO. NY - 1983

This beach was far different from the Montauk site. The sand was deep and loose. I put my pick-up into four-wheel, always starting in second gear because of the truck's high torque. Off I went, from the pavement to the sand. I ran through second gear way too quickly, shifted into third and struggled to a spot twenty feet from the dunes. My F-250 was a powerful vehicle, and I couldn't understand why it performed so poorly on the sand. I came across a fellow beach camper and asked for some advice. He knew the answer immediately and told me I was running with too much air in my tires. "Drive with thirty pounds of air, not the seventy you're running with now."

Having low air pressure in your tires gives it a wider base, which equates to a floating balloon-like feel. His advice worked like a charm. The only downfall is when I had to exit onto the pavement to buy food. There was a free-use air pump at the point where the sand transitioned to blacktop. Problem

Smith Point - Beach Camping

was, to use the air pump, you needed to have your own portable hose to hook up. I did not have the equipment. That was okay. It wasn't a far distance from the major boulevard. On the way home, it was different since I had to travel about a mile to find a service station to fill my tires for the ride home.

Before I purchased my 1983 F-250 truck, I took my first trip out to Montauk with Jimbo and Pete, a neighborhood guy who was not in our circle of friends. He had a 1982 F-250 automatic. We ventured out completely unprepared, figuring that once we got there, we would find some woods and sleep in the cab and bed of the truck. Paying for a hotel room in Montauk was well beyond our means. We arrived and drove around the small village, checking out the place. We discovered a wooded lot to park and sleep. Pete slept on the bench seat in comfort, Jimbo and I slept in sleeping bags in the truck's bed. Bare bones comfort was not the reason for us being there — it was strictly for the adventure. We knew where a drugstore was from our recon the day before. We bought some cheap, see-through tourist towels and a tube of toothpaste. In the village parking lot, we finger brushed and rinsed with the "king of beers."

On our way to anywhere, we saw a sign with an arrow that said, "horse tours" and thought it would be cool to take a guided ride through a wooded area and onto the beach. It was my first time on a horse, and it scared the shit out of me. Until you are in the saddle, you can't appreciate the power of the animal. Along with the three of us, there were others, including the woman who was our guide. We started off on trails through the woods at a walking pace. Quickly, it progressed to full-blown, ride 'em cowboy style. I was in survival mode, just trying to keep my butt in the saddle as these powerful beauties were running much faster than I expected. Then, the shit hit the fan. Pete's horse, who was second to the guides, did a "Hi-Ho -Silver" and off Pete went to the right. He landed hard on his right hand, breaking his wrist. I could tell he was hurting, but he wanted to continue for the duration of the ride.

The second half of the tour was mellow, horses calm, sauntering on the beach. Taking in the ocean views on horseback was something that I always wanted to do. We came upon three guys who immediately started mouthing off to the guide. They were going on and on about the horses defecating on the beach and they wanted her and the horses gone. It got quite heated. Jimbo was itching to fight. Hell, I'll back him up, but I had no beef here. He asked the guide if she wanted him to tune up these three. Cooler heads prevailed, and we continued on. Discussing situations through was more my style. I liked Jimbo, but he was always too eager to get into a fight. On the west side of the Kensico Dam, in Jimbo's hometown, he tangled with a black belt at a bar. I was not present. He was badly beaten and hospitalized. Steve and I visited him; he was asleep with both hands holding onto his family jewels. I assumed he got kicked there — a lot.

Horse time was over, and Pete needed to get to the community hospital to have his wrist taken care of. In three years, I paid a visit there. He came out with a cast on. I was driving an old, beat-up Chevy pickup. Pete knew I could handle his truck and threw me the keys. Cool, I was thinking about getting a new one exactly like this with a standard shift. That long drive home served as the ultimate test drive. Shortly after, I bought mine.

Chapter 16

The Boat

A favorite run of mine was navigating the often-tricky waters under Hell Gate Rail Bridge, making a stop at LaGuardia Airport, to catch a few planes landing, then onward to the Whitestone Bridge.

That was always my terminus. I wasn't much of a Long Island Sound guy. Nothing there ever piqued my interest. I captained a friend's vessel through Hell Gate from New Rochelle on a night run, so he could become accustomed on his return and future trips.

Hell Gate Rail Bridge - NYC - 1984

My 1969, 16 foot Glastron, powered by a 1972, 150 hp Evinrude, took me places I dreamed of as a preteen. Cruising the waters of NYC and the Hudson Highlands were the most exhilarating times of my life. Working from 8am to 3:30pm afforded me an afternoon cruise nearly every day until dusk. The city was a quick trip from Yonkers, southbound on the Hudson, where I would enter the Harlem River, pass under the swiveling rail bridge, always looking out for the dreaded Circle Line. Forget about yielding to a smaller vessel. I was a bug to their captain.

On an ordinary summer afternoon, Crazy JJ and I were lounging, bow pointed across from the iconic Columbia University "C" painted on the Bronx-side rock face at the river's edge.

Columbia U. - 'C' - Bronx, NY - 1984

Oh, shit, here she comes, the flipping Circle Line, as usual, exceeding her speed limit, which meant that we were in for a wake, soaking moment. It hit us hard. We were baptized with the tasty river water when my bow popped upward and crashed down.

My first trip, before my buddy Joe painted her, was a run around Manhattan starting at the Harlem River, down to the southern section of the East River, a loop around Lady Liberty, hugging the Palisades to the Tappan Zee Bridge.

Joe taught me the basics, enough to keep me alive on the water. He painted her completely black, even the windshield. I always captained my vessel with my leg tucked under my butt to see floating debris. I hit a lot of cast-off pieces of pilings, especially at midtown on the Hudson, and a memorable, huge, telephone pole that was bobbing in the muddy waters of the Harlem River. The pole appeared fifteen feet dead ahead, and there was nothing I could do but drive over it and hope it hit my motor's lower end square so it would pop up and not damage my propeller. I was lucky. Everything worked out fine.

I usually tore down the Harlem with everything that Evinrude had with no incidents. There is a point where the Harlem meets the East River and, just when you pass Carl Schurz Park and round the point, the skyscrapers suddenly overwhelm you.

Being low in the water makes it an even more spectacular sight, that I loved to share with newcomers on my boat. All the bridges around Manhattan were cool to travel under, but nothing beats the Brooklyn Bridge. That is as fine as it gets. I always slowed her down and took in as much as I could from a

Hell Gate Rail Bridge - NYC - 1984

respite at Pier 17. The East River was rough at times. I usually hugged the Manhattan side, where I could find calm water.

On one of my runs down to the city, I changed my usual route of entering at the Harlem River. There was a large ship in the distance, just below midtown, and I stayed my course on the Hudson. I caught up to a Cunard ocean liner — dressed in its black hull with white from its deck up. Seeing an opportunity to do some surfing, I came within two hundred feet of the liner's stern and aimed for its port side wake, which was about four feet high. I throttled to the crest of the wake, surfed a bit, then full throttled her, back north to Yonkers.

Following a late spring afternoon of boating, just as I was heading toward my slip, I sighted a long shape down river. I yelled to JJ, "it looks like a body." The creamy white object was floating, motionless, on the calm water. Uncharacteristically, I wasn't reluctant to head toward it. As we came closer, we realized it was way too big to be human — it was an enormous fish. I told JJ to grab the oar and bring it alongside the boat. We gave it a measure against my sixteen-foot-long vessel. The giant was two feet shy of my boat's length. JJ rolled the fish over, revealing the markings of an extraordinary creation — the Atlantic Sturgeon, a fourteen foot long, prehistoric looking beauty. It was plain to see that a propeller gash on its top midsection caused its death. No bloating was evident, which led us to conclude that we were upon a recent kill. This beautiful animal was making its way upriver to spawn. I can only imagine how many times that magnificent creature had lumbered up the majestic Hudson. We let it be, to be consumed by nature.

The farthest north that I ventured on the Hudson was two runs to the vicinity of Marlboro, NY, sixty miles from home. Traveling that far from home base, Yonkers was always fraught with possibilities of mechanical failure. I made a habit of bringing a tool kit, spare prop, oar, and plenty of spark plugs, along with enough fuel and oil. I crammed in three large portable cans, totaling sixteen gallons, and topped off at marinas along the way. That was the extent of my smarts. In the early eighties, communication was by radio, which I could not afford. I knew my landmarks, noting each bridge that I passed under. I cruised by the seat of my pants, just knowing enough to point into the wake of an oncoming, larger vessel. Overnight camp-outs were fabulous, also nerve-wracking. Securing the boat perpendicular to the rough beach had its challenges. Setting the anchor isn't always a one-shot task. Once accomplished, the stern line was cake. There was the dreaded swim out into the cold Hudson the next morning, praying that she would start. I always camped on the eastern shore by a railroad track. My thought process was, if the boat doesn't start, I could always walk the tracks and find civilization.

I received the call at 7am, from Mr. M, Joe's father, who was the marina owner and dockmaster. He informed me that her bow was still tied, showing three feet above the waterline. My rear cleats were gone. My nameless vessel took on heavy water at the dock during a late-night storm. I covered her well, but the strong winds breached her canvas. I had her equipped with a bilge pump but did not keep the battery onboard. The dock was not in the best of neighborhoods, but I should have checked on her that stormy night. If I only left that house party in Valhalla, she could have been saved. My bud JJ loaded my truck with chains, rope, five-gallon bucket, hand-truck, and an engine hoist.

I got into the water and secured a line, rigged up a chain/rope combo, and connected to the extended hoist that JJ had lashed to the fixed dock. He cranked that hoist just enough for the stern to get a few inches above the water. I bailed for hours. The river took everything inside the boat. When I got her stable, with a foot of water remaining, JJ jumped in and severed all lines to the outboard. We cranked that motor out and strapped it to a heavy-duty U-Haul hand-truck. I walked my wounded Glastron one hundred feet to the entrance of the dock. The only way out for her was a hull ripping trip over the shoreline rock wall. My truck pulled her out with ease. She gave me and my buds six months of delight.

Thirty-nine years later, I can still feel my body floating, being pulled southbound, as I looked up at West Point. To be in and experience the power of the river — how fortunate and blessed I was.

Chapter 17

Digit

I turned around and headed towards the calmer waters of the Harlem River that I had exited a half hour prior. I was near the United Nations building, where the waters of the East River were too rough that summer day. A moment after my reversal, I saw a New York City police boat approaching me on my starboard side. Nothing seemed unusual. I knew they tied up a few of their vessels in the Harlem River at a dock alongside one of the small bridges that connect the Bronx and Manhattan. The orders emanating from a loudspeaker to slow my speed abruptly ended my assumption that we had mutual routes. I complied with the order and quickly a massive police boat, which resembled a tugboat, was alongside me. A police officer shouted for me to follow him towards the wall at the East River Drive. I followed him for about fifty yards. He appeared on deck and gave me direct instructions about what was to happen next.

At that moment, I did not know why I was being pulled over. My vessel was a ski boat with an arched, stainless tow bar at the stern. Below the gunwales were deep, long slots that accommodated skis. I had one stored, and the rest of the two compartments were packed with empty Budweiser cans. They were all just an accumulation of laziness. My first thought was, when the officer sees all the beer cans, he is going to test me for a DUI. I wasn't drinking that day and when I did; it was responsibly. Instruction time commenced. I was ten feet from that enormous vessel and the officer yelled to me, "I'm going to point my boat perpendicular to this granite wall, then I am going to give half power to keep me pinned against it. Once you see me stationary, I want you to come around and tie-up to me on my port side." OK, now the pieces were coming together. He wanted to board my boat for some sort of inspection. This behemoth had her engine engaged and was creating a lot of churning at its stern. I thought it would be best to stay clear of that hazard, so I swung out wide and came back in for my tie up. That sharply painted New York City blue and orange ship shadowed my craft.

I was thinking about interjecting a little humor into our encounter and say, "yes, permission granted to come aboard, sir." I thought better and kept my pie hole shut. The officer climbed down into my boat. This was not my first rodeo with the police. They had pulled me over quite a few times on land, but never on the water. "Keep your cool, be respectful, swirled throughout my head." I assumed his next words would be for me to produce my license and registration. I was correct and gathered what he requested. He looked and returned my credentials. His next request was to see my fire extinguisher, life jackets, and anchor. I bracketed my extinguisher at the port stern and instructed him to peek under the front seats where he could see the jackets. My anchor was beside my seat. I was expecting him to do a field sobriety test on me. That was not performed. He could tell that I was not drinking. I was wondering, what next? Is this guy just messing with me? "OK, Mr. Waitzman, here's the reason I'm detaining you. You're missing a number on the side of your boat." "I said to myself, we have a first-class asshole here. He has a primo job on the force, cruising the waters of NYC daily." I looked over the starboard side and saw a vinyl number missing. He wrote me out a ticket and instructed me to leave before him. Well, that was one for the record books. "Strange police pull-overs."

I had to appear in court to answer the violation. That meant a day missed from work. I worked for a contractor. If you don't show, you don't get paid. To add insult to a pay loss, I had to find a parking lot and pay their exorbitant fee. I made my way to the narrow, long Manhattan courtroom. Fortunately, it had benches. There were many people in front of me. After two hours, my name was called, and I stood in front of the judge. He told me to give the bailiff my license and registration. "Mr. Waitzman, have you replaced the missing number on your boat?" Yes, sir, I have. "Good, you are free to go." I was expecting to pay a fine. The judge said nothing more, and I didn't ask. My fine was a day's pay and parking. I know the officer was doing his job. In my opinion, it was an unnecessary exercise on his part. C'est la vie.

Chapter 18

Bob

I was searching through my old files and came across a brief Facebook post with Bob.

3/28 1:09pm What's up buddy? Steve sent me a lead to a friend request from you. We're both still here in the world. I'm hitting the bed early tonight, so get a message to me and we can catch up, old partner.

3/28 5:22pm Yup, Bob, we had fun working together at Sciullo. You were a great partner! We got shit done. Good, fun memories. I saw your tool belt hanging on your profile pic. Done for good, eh? What have you been up to? Steve told me you got married a while ago. I left the Big YO in '93 and live across the river from Charleston. Earned a graphics degree and have been working in that field since '99. Love it here. Historical interests are everywhere and NO snow. I recall you telling me that your mom was with the Yonkers Historical Society. Am I right with that? She would have liked this area. That's my life, post NY, in a nutshell. Let me know what's going on with you.

3/29 3:21pm What's up Jimbo? Good to hear from you. I think about you and the fun we used to have. Nobody has any fun at work anymore, it's just work now, so I said screw-it and hung up my tools. Good to hear from you. Hope all is well by you.

Bob was a Northwest Yonkers guy, seven years my senior. His carpenter local was Yonkers, mine was White Plains. When we worked together at Sciullo Construction, our job sites were mostly in and around White Plains. In the early 1980s, we didn't feel the recession, work was plentiful. We were fortunate to be hooked up with contractors that secured bids at the many corporations headquartered in Westchester County. Sciullo locked up a lot of the Citibank renovations, along with an office building in Armonk and his spec building on the site of the old White Plains dump. The thousands of glass bottles that the backhoe scooped were time capsule treasures. We filled many five-gallon buckets with the primo ones. I still have an assortment displayed on the sill of my half round office window.

When I knew Bob, he lived a spartan existence in a house apartment in rough, south-central Yonkers. He was an honest guy, who loved and told a good joke. We gelled well together at work. He had excellent communication skills, and we became a well-oiled machine. We cut, fitted and screwed-off fire code compliant boards around I-beams in commercial buildings. There was pride in our work. We were both of the same mindset — do it correctly or don't do it at all. On a job site in Port Chester, Herb was the grumpy supervisor. He would spend his day sitting at a desk in the center of the unfinished second-floor slab. His only conversation with us was how to create the perfect Swedish wood filler. His lesson was appreciated. Bob was determined to get him to laugh. Pointing across the street, Bob asked,

"Herb, are you familiar with Don Bosco Parish?" "Sure, I see it every day." "Then you must know that Don Bosco is the patron saint of chocolate milk." Herb roared with an explosive belly laugh. Bob was pleased. Laughter knocked down the walls between us for the remainder of that job.

For a season, we played men's softball together in the Thornwood Water District League. He was a decent player with a lot of heart and hustle, which elevated his game. Bob always declined invites for an after-work cruise on my boat that was tied up down the hill from his place. He would simply say, "Jimbo, I don't care for boats." He agreed to go on a weekend cabin stay with me and the tapers upstate, near Cooperstown. We had a blast riding the snowmobile through the forest trails in the late winter. Bob was content sipping a cold one as he chain-smoked from the porch of the cabin.

I miss our morning coffee together, discussing the previous afternoon's showing of Love Connection. At day's end, he would flash the victory sign, rotating his "V" from front to back, just like host Chuck Woolery did before a commercial break. Bob's Facebook profile photo displayed his worn tool belt. He made it clear that he was through with the trade — then, with his life. I'm hoping that he will buckle his tool belt and use it when we meet on the other side.

Chapter 19

The Circuit

I was traveling with my golf comadre, on Shore Road in New Rochelle, NY, and we crossed into Bronx County, NY, where there once was a large, cleared lot on the immediate left — about the same square footage as half of a football field. Locally, it was referred to as "prostitute point," which I never understood. Not once did I or my friends see a prostitute there; just fifty-five-gallon drum "warmth fires," beer-pounding gatherings, family picnics, cars being worked on — the usual stuff. The name was just an urban myth.

Some years back, an NYC-DOT road crew sealed the place off, installing four hundred feet of guard rail. Other than memories — weeds, saplings, and scarred-ice-age, coastal rock are all that remains. This was the local route that I was introduced to on my first trip into the massive Pelham Bay Park, New York City's largest. The more traveled, popular access is via the Hutchinson River Parkway. Left at the City Island traffic circle, the well-worn, poorly lit, Turtle Cove mini-golf and driving range can be found. We played numerous rounds, gripping the billions of bacteria that lived on those rental putter hand grips. They had to furnish us some immunity benefit.

After a workout at the links, Nina and I always headed to the attractively lit and tastefully appointed City Island. She exclusively ordered fried clam strips, fries, and an unknown beverage — you'd think I'd know a friend's beverage of choice after eight years. Completing that mini course always left us equally hungry. The last joint on the right provided a seafood platter reward that was well deserved. I must mention that my great friend, who is a multi-subject conversationalist, funny and equally sarcastic, ranks a numero uno in my book. She was a solid friend then and now.

Second up on our summer of 1985 mini-golf circuit was Playland, fifteen miles north on I-95. Playland mini-golf could be intimidating, with its crowds and bright lights. It had grass that was smoother, and the borders were modern and true. They sent pairs out quickly, which took a bit of the leisurely fun away. You had to be on your game at "the land" or the sugar and carb-loaded crowds would get harsh. After our play on the links, my customary show-off maneuver was the pitching speed gun — yeah, you know it, where the former high school hurler, who had a few clocked in the low 90s, attempts the same results. It beckoned me. I couldn't resist. My shoulder was always sore on the job come Monday morning. Playland had the great rides, the art deco motif, and no gum stuck to the ground. The place had class.

The last two courses on the circuit were on a nondescript stretch of Central Avenue, that I had visited regularly since age 11. First of the last loops was newer, plain, with newness being its only attribute. The last and oldest on the circuit needed some love. It was bohemian and dripping with character. That multi-leveled gem on a steep hillside had patches of plastic turf missing, that were replaced with hard rubber. You had to come up with imaginative ways to negotiate your path to the cup. Fun and funky, I preferred this last remaining survivor in the area. Nina was a diehard fan of Turtle Cove. I would estimate that we played twenty rounds at those little pieces of paradise that spring and summer of 1985.

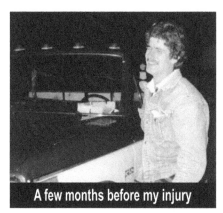

A few months before my injury

My second-to-last visit to Playland was at sister Ellie's, "Einstein Hospital Family Day." My return after my injury was not as emotionally difficult as I had imagined. We were inside a huge pavilion, next to the park's bumper cars. My last visit to Playland was with my two nephews — I was driving again and had to park in the far north end, which I had never done before. The boys enjoyed the rides and their multiple attempts to shoot out the paper star. We had a fabulous time. As I started up my accessible 1991 Ford van — on cue — the theme song from The Band's, *"The Last Waltz"* began. What a sweet memory of that symphonic arrangement, with its beautiful, haunting strings that had touched my soul. I could not have planned a more exquisite farewell. I slowly circled around the vast parking lot until the last note. I then returned the ether to the night air for fulfillment of others.

Chapter 20

Buddy

"You two have been calling each other buddy all day, what's up with that?"

"We say buddy, buddeee, and depending on the circumstance, we throw in a few expletives before or after. You never call a friend, buddy?"

"No, never — a Jamaican would never call a friend, buddy."

"And why is that?"

"Because buddy translates to penis."

"Ah, so you think that we've been calling each other a dick all day?"

"Yes," said the new carpenter hire at a Citibank branch where Steve, George, and I were working. Steve was a member of the Yonkers local; George and I were out of White Plains. Our Jamaican carpentry brother was sent to the job site from my local to balance out the number of White Plains carpenters on the build. Steve and I refer to each other as buddy to this day.

I first met Steve on a job site in Greenwich, Connecticut, in 1981. I had been working for Tri-State Interiors as a non-union apprentice for a year and a half. Steve was hired out of the Yonkers local by my boss Carl, who was building office space at Ridge Hill in Yonkers, just behind the old tuberculosis sanitarium on the ridge adjacent to the New York State Thruway. When that job was completed, our paths crossed, and a friendship was formed that has lasted over forty years. Steve is a master carpenter and took me under his wing. Aside from work, we had and have much in common. We are both Yonkers natives, share a love of family, Italian food, sports, and love to mess with each other. Working on scissor lifts, with a load of four by twelve sheetrock onboard, thirty feet up is not my idea of fun. Buddy relished in scaring the crap out of me — either dancing on the lift, standing on the safety rails while shooting a powder-actuated nail into an I-beam or driving the lift while at maximum height. Those warehouse builds were nerve-racking; framing heavy gauge steel and screwing-off long sheets of drywall.

Steve and his wife, Maryellen, have raised four lovely children. I was bestowed the honor of being godfather to their oldest daughter, Dayna. I made it to all their baptismal celebrations before my time in Yonkers ran its course.

I eventually became a union carpenter and continued working with Steve at Tri-State. We worked at a vast number of IBM facilities, with 1133 Westchester Avenue serving as a quasi-home base. Tri-State was owned by Tony and Carl, two decent men who broke me into the trade. We worked many contract and time and material jobs at IBM. Buddy and I danced in the elevators, and slid into imaginary bases on the highly polished, asbestos laden tiles. We zoomed large wall panels through the vast corridors upon our well-worn "A" frame transport rack. Most contract jobs were done after hours. The bosses always sent Steve out, where he fulfilled our dinner requests with a wad of cash from Tony. We ate well. Buddy would bring back hot subs and assorted peppers that would curl your hair. We always got a kick out of Carl, sweating profusely from the spicy selections.

Steve had decided to move on to another outfit and I soon followed. It was similar work, with a change of corporate venue from IBM to Citibank.

We came back on several occasions to work after hours for Tri-State. These jobs involved building walls above the ceiling grid, where the asbestos loomed. We regularly removed and replaced worn ceiling tiles and riveted channels to the ceiling grid, which encompassed the extent of our above ceiling work. These new, above the ceiling jobs were now strictly mon-

Steve and me

itored, involving a certified asbestos company that required us to build multiple decontamination stations. If you needed to use the restroom, your hooded PPE garb had to be vacuumed off before it was removed, tools and tool belt cleaned, and your respirator had to be checked. Those paper-thin suits were hot as hell. We stripped down to our briefs when wearing them. In those days, I changed my facial hair style frequently. Mustache, goatee, and full beard were all in my rotation. When it came to fitting the respirator properly, the facial hair had to go — tight seals were paramount. We even duct taped the suits at our ankles. After four jobs into the hazardous realm of asbestos, Steve was no longer willing to risk his health, and I wholeheartedly agreed. The money wasn't worth the potential damage to our lungs.

Part of my job description on contract jobs was to load the demolition truck and drive it up to the Croton dump. Once you checked in at the weigh station, the inspector took your card and entered it into the computer, along with the truck's entry weight. He always asked if my load was garbage or clean demo. I was always hauling clean demo, which had a designated dump site. Sometimes, they would check my load through the side doors or the top of the hydraulic rear gate.

The clean demo area didn't mean that you were exempt from the stench of every rotting, earthly thing imaginable in a dump. Getting to the top of this huge mound of human waste was always an interesting, scary trip. The road near the top was constantly being altered from the previous day's volume. There was always a consistent, slippery passageway that teetered on the hill's edge, cut by enormous bulldozers with steel-spiked front and rear drum-like wheels. Every crest attempt required a full throttled run from base to summit. That 1968 Ford truck had reached its expiration date long ago, but it never bogged down and left me stuck. The vehicle did not hydraulically dump its load — it was a piece by piece, hand unload, which took two hours. I emptied the load and drove back down the garbage mountain, much lighter and craving a beverage. I always bought Yoo-Hoo, Fanta orange and a Dr. Pepper, which I pounded down in the 7-Eleven parking lot.

A memorable dump run with Steve had us taking an eastern, detoured route to his newly purchased home in Yorktown Heights for a dip in the pool before heading down to White Plains to join our bosses. This was Steve and Maryellen's first home after moving from their apartment in Yonkers. They fixed up that small Cape Cod house to their liking and worked hard for a larger home. After a few years at Sciullo construction company, Steve went out on his own. It was summer, and I had the option of joining Steve and Maryellen for a long weekend at the Jersey shore or my friend Joe at the Hamptons for a farewell dinner before his move to California. I knew that seeing Joe again would be far in the future. I chose to go to the Hamptons, where I was injured.

Steve and Maryellen visited me quite a bit when I was at rehab in Manhattan. They included me in their lives, and I am darn grateful. Early in my injury, Steve brought me to a Met game at Big Shea against my beloved Cubs. We were upper decking it. Buddy lifted me from my wheelchair and carried me up a dozen steps, placed my cushion on the blue plastic seat, and gently placed me down. Before I started driving my adaptive van, buddy would make the drive from Yorktown Heights to Yonkers, pick me up, drive me back up and back home after a family celebration. I enjoyed seeing Steve and Maryellen pre-pandemic, here in Mount Pleasant. Distance separates us, but not in our hearts.

Chapter 21

My New Four Letter Word

I have entered the belly of the beast. I know it's a worn out cliche. At that moment, for me, it was à propos. I am still strapped to a gurney, with my head and neck immobilized, and some sort of weights are dangling off the back of my head for support. I'm being rushed to the ICU in Bellevue Hospital. I have heard stories about this iconic, fabulous, filthy place. The good news was, I knew, like most who live in the New York City metro area, that I was in a top-notch trauma hospital. Unfortunately, I fit the criteria. This is where my hospital nightmare began.

In the ICU, I'm suddenly in the comfort of my family members. They had to be in shock. Later into the night, I can't recall when, one of my sisters told me that daddy was speaking to the doctor and said, "you have to make him well, he's just like me." In some ways, I was like my father but, in most ways, I didn't come close. My father, God rest his soul, as well as my mother, are wonderful people. They were depression-era kids. My mother had a difficult early childhood, losing her father at seven years old, and growing up poor. She happily made her way out of Pittsfield, MA, and eventually started her nursing career in NYC.

She worked as an operating room nurse, then spent many years working the graveyard shift at Graham School, Saturday at the methadone clinic, closing out her career in the clinic at North General in Manhattan. My father was the son of a rising executive at American Bakeries. He left Cornell University to enlist in the army in WWII, where he served as a radio operator, strike caller in the 292nd JASCO Division. He was in many locations in the Pacific Theater. His career was in wholesale auto parts, and he then transitioned to the export of parts to the Middle East. My parents raised three boys and three girls. They both were and are selfless parents.

I was hearing talk of a device that I had never heard of — the HALO. After a considerable time had passed, I barely see a nurse carrying what looked like a medieval torture device. It was headed my way. I had more curiosity than fear. The nurse explained that this nearly circular steel piece of medical equipment was going to be placed over the top of my head and screwed into my forehead, as well as the rear of my head. Yes, screwed with an actual, slotted screwdriver. This was the most surreal moment of my life thus far. First, multiple shots of some sort of numbing agent were injected at four points, then they screwed the halo into my head. I could hear the crackling of my skull.

With all the numbing injections, you would think that there couldn't possibly be any pain. Well, there certainly was. After all, four screws were in, four rods were attached to clamps on the halo, then they were attached to a hard plastic shell that started at my breast plate and ended at my lower ribcage. It's on. My neck is completely void of movement. I'm a human battering ram. This device certainly took a while to get used to. My eyes strained daily, panning left to right. To add to this new joy, two major components of this device were attached incorrectly. The halo was installed too close to the back of my head, which caused my first pressure sore that eventually healed, leaving a gash where hair will never grow again. The hard shell left its mark as well. My left scapula developed a pressure sore too. You would think that being admitted into one of New York's premier trauma hospitals, they would know how to put this device on properly.

After a few weeks in the ICU, they moved me to the floor in Bellevue. On a routine check, late at night, a resident noticed that the right screw in my forehead was loose and damaged, needing replacement immediately. The resident injected novocaine and then used the screwdriver for the replacement. He turned the new screw at a slightly different area, about 1/4 inch from the original site. As he turned the screwdriver, the familiar bone crackling began. This time was considerably more painful. I was screaming. It hurt me terribly. The resident said to me, "come on, it can't be that painful." I couldn't believe his callousness. I angrily told him to keep his mouth shut and do his job. My survival mode was at the maximum level. I never saw that prick again.

I wore this uncomfortable hunk of hardware for three and a half months. Sleeping was the worst part of the day. Comfort of any kind was unattainable. My fabulous family and my fantastic friend Nina were always visiting, usually after 5pm. Without their support, I would not have survived. Nina and Lisa cooked many meals for my family. Nina always brought flowers when visiting. I'm happy that we keep in contact with each other.

The day that torture device was removed, I cried tears of joy. My neck muscles were so atrophied, it felt like my head was going to fall off my shoulders. They fitted me with a hard Philadelphia collar for a few weeks to allow for my neck muscles to get back into a strengthened state. When I had my halo removed, I was well into my stay at NYU Rusk Rehabilitation, commonly known as "Bedpan Row," because of the many hospitals on the street. The nurses were excellent — they taught me everything I needed to know about living a life with a spinal cord injury. They made me name every medication before they were administered. The nurses liked to joke around a lot to keep our spirits up. Once, a nurse brought in those sponge-like animal toys that expand when you put them in water. They delighted in pushing the toy onto the end of our halo screws.

My roomie Don, my man, was a kindred spirit. We had mirrored similarities in work and interests. I liked him a lot. He was in rehab months before I arrived and was two months post halo. Don never went to therapy like the rest of us. When I asked him to come and join us, he looked at me and said, "really man, what's the fucking use?" I did get him to an occupational therapy session one afternoon. "Don, there's a babe named Jane who just started working here." I sealed the deal when I told him she usually wore a tight black leather jacket. Those of us that could, would catch or swat the beach ball, Don would hit the ball with his head to keep it in play. He never returned to an occupational therapy class. He thanked me for the afternoon of some serious eye candy. Pete, who I keep in virtual contact with, informed me that Don left us in the 1990s. I don't have any knowledge of Johnny. I hope he is in good health and enjoying his mom's cooking, his children, and the movies.

Across the hall from the occupational therapy room, locked behind a heavy wooden door, was a computer. It was brought out into the room and patients were invited to learn about it. In 1980, I was aware of computers. Before my injury, I saw my sister, who worked at IBM staring and typing on a computer keyboard all day. I wanted no part of that.When encouraged to learn, my standard response was, "no, why would I want to do that?"

I am truly blessed

Quite ironic that I currently make my living and enjoy creating, using a computer. The halo, the apparatus that stabilized my cervical spine through my healing process, gave me more benefit than the physically obvious. During my time, trapped in its clutches, forced me to cultivate my mental strength. It was difficult, but I succeeded. Those were rough days; nights were worse.

Chapter 22

IF to WHEN

"IF" expresses a wish and "WHEN" a resolve. After my cervical injury, there were many IFs. Medically, the IFs were overwhelming. At Bellevue Hospital, they gave me an experimental drug to reduce the swelling at the injury site of my spinal cord. Swelling leads to damaging expansion of the spinal cord. There was hope that IF the swelling was reduced, more precious nerves would remain intact. Retaining any body functions, including bowel and bladder, would be a life changing IF.

When I was given the experimental drug, my sister Ellie attempted a little bribery. The drug was most likely coded, so no one administering it would detect results until the end of the controlled study. That long shot IF, rolled into tiny little snake eyes. Was I given the placebo or the real deal? I never found out; it didn't matter. If the drug had been successful, results would have been published — the world would know. Breakthroughs in SCI get noticed quickly.

When I arrived at Room 405, I was in a corner bed with no window, which was depressing. My original roommates were Dennis, who was a missionary, injured in Central America, injury level C2, with no movement below his neck. Don and Johnny were the same level as Dennis. Johnny became my left-hand man when I moved to Dennis' old window spot. My new view with a precious, clear blue sky brought my spirits up. Johnny had first dibs, but he was comfortable in his corner. He lived in Brooklyn, took Friday afternoon through Sunday night weekend passes home in gypsy cabs. He loved his mother's cooking, his family, and he could be alone with his wife and two kids. Johnny and his brother loved the movies and would hit the theaters that showed the horror flicks.

Now, we're talking well before the Americans with Disabilities Act. Johnny and his brother navigated through NYC when there were no curb cuts and no elevators to the trains. I admired him. He was living! He arrived at his salvage yard job and a garage door fell on his neck. We were all in the demographic for spinal cord injury — age sixteen through twenty-five, mostly male. Don was a party animal. He would go out with the nurses after their Friday shift and hit the clubs. When the nurses had to leave, Don would stay. A nurse would find someone and Don always got back to rehab by 7am. I never saw when he returned, but I heard from the staff that Don was smoking by the elevators and feeling fine. He shared his technique on how to extinguish a cigarette. "Jim, all you have to do is this, if you don't want to catch yourself on fire — that's a horrible way to go." I surely agreed as Don gathered up enough saliva on his tongue and rolled his steamed cigarette onto the wet side, got it fully extinguished, and spat it on the floor. Simple and effective.

Johnny had his boom box volume low enough that it was hardly detectable. At night, when our room was quiet and we all longed for our past lives, I first heard the song *"Hold Me"* from Johnny's cassette tape. I knew the male vocal was Teddy Pendergrass, who suffered a spinal cord injury a few years prior to ours. I asked Johnny, who's the woman vocal? "She's new. Her name is Whitney Houston. I love her, she'll go far with those pipes." She sure did, God rest her soul. Our last member of the Fighting 405th was John Wayne-loving Peter, who couldn't get enough of "The Duke." The head nurse removed his framed photo off the top of his light ledge. Can you imagine that? Nurse ratchet confiscated my small boom box too, claiming that it did not have the required, certified approval from the institution's electrician. We had few possessions to enjoy, and they were being picked off one by one. That heartless SOB gave us no slack. She returned my music after we all raised hell. If "Joe College" was permitted to enjoy his VCR in his private room across the hallway from us, then it was everyone's right to electronics or no one's. Music was an important part of our rehab.

One week before going home from rehab, the NYU hospital psychologist entered my room once more and asked what I did in occupational therapy class. I showed her and she made a comment that was not appreciated. She wanted to know how I felt, how I really felt. We had covered this delicate area before. "How could I answer that question?" I don't yet know. I grabbed the piece of card stock, on which I had drawn a rough plan of a ski chalet. I clumsily shook it in front of her and said that I felt proud, pleased — can you not see my joy? How I felt was intermingled with accomplishment. The coordination I developed with my new orthotic, in conjunction with my remaining arm function, produced a satisfying drawing. That was a monumental WHEN! I have used that style of brace to eat, write and draw for over thirty-seven years.

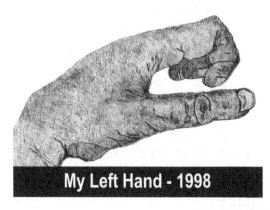

My Left Hand - 1998

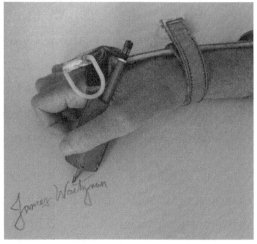

I have worn the leather out of dozens. The morning of my scheduled departure from the Rusk Institute in Manhattan, I was begged by this same employee to stay for the matinee of "Sexuality and Quadriplegia." After denying her multiple attempts, I got blunt with her. "I know you are well intentioned, but right now I am going home to put my life back into some semblance of order." My game plan was a tiny IF. I could only do this with the help of my family. I made a promise with myself to see a psychologist if I felt I could no longer mentally cope with this catastrophic injury. The last thing I was thinking of doing at that moment was to view quads screwing.

I surely understood that sexuality was a part of life. At that stage of my injury, it was not in my playbook.

I saw my favorite NYU Rusk Rehab employee upon exit. After hugging my PTs, OTs, nurses and CNAs, the head nurse received the back of my head. We loathed her. She was the one who didn't care for our beloved music at any volume. On an afternoon of down time, me and the boys got a bit revved up and played "Brothers in Arms," by Dire Straits — loudly. Peter, who bunked diagonally from me, the captain of the "Fighting 405th," gave the order. None of us had served, but we shared the similar quadriplegic experience, and became brothers.

In 1992, a big IF involved cooling the spinal injury site directly and quickly, with two medicines. This benefited NY Jets lineman Dennis Byrd tremendously. He regained nearly complete function. That medical cocktail was developed at The Miami Project to Cure Paralysis, where dad, mom and I traveled to in 1987. I took part in a one-year Functional Electrical Stimulation (FES) study of the lower and upper body. I gained a small increase in wrist function, that was labeled as non-functional, but gained a substantial increase in leg muscle mass in the study, and from a home use ERGYS bike. That WHEN went kaput due to the friction while riding. First my skin was damaged, then the sacral area, primarily my tailbone. The tailbone became gelatinous and was removed — best body part that was ever 86ed. I believe we have evolved from the need for a tail.

Mt. Vernon hospital had an experimental program, primarily intended for diabetics. Our pharmacist gave us the info, and I was quickly in the **Procuren** program. My wound healed in 1/4 the time of a conventional flap surgery — a big WHEN. We felt good about our experience in Miami — we gave and worked for a cause that will ultimately end many forms of suffering and render paralysis to a blip from the past. Many family members and friends donate to the cause, for which I am grateful. One day, most likely not in my lifetime, that IF will become a monumental WHEN.

Early in my quad life, I had to build back the pride in myself that I had possessed as an able-bodied man. I had a difficult time with my new shyness. I believe the turning point was when I learned how to drive an accessible van. My parents brought up the idea and encouraged me. At first, it scared me. I didn't want to hurt anyone or myself. That was a huge IF that I worked on and cultivated to a Kick-Ass WHEN. It changed my new, paralyzed, static life into a tremendous independence, giving me a treasured freedom.

Driving down the highway, the occasional yahoo would beep at me because I was not driving at their preferred speed. I often said to myself, "yeah jackass, can you pull this off? I don't think so." Just affirming with myself in my new — old head. When I parked my polished-up van and unloaded myself, then tore-ass in my chair to wherever I wanted to go — that was a feeling, a damn good feeling. In 1992, when I received my service dog, Lee, he enhanced the pride in myself even more. Now I could keep a dog under control properly and tool around, most anywhere I chose.

My new life and my folks needed to find a fresh start. We found it in South Carolina, after my younger sister Pat moved there with her family. We moved into a new apartment for three years while I went to school, earning an associate in commercial graphics. I would have loved to study in Savannah, but it was over a hundred miles south of us, and their curriculum at the time involved more physicality than I could muster. Along with that, I need nearly 24/7 on my body functions. That's a lot of coin. I landed a job a few days out of college. After opening my book to page two, the boss said that he didn't need to see any more. "The reality is, I can't pay you that much." I said, "no problem, I'll part time it, that's all I have in me." That job lasted for ten years. I had been unemployed for several years when I heard of an opening at a business looking for a social media guy. I was employed by a cruise franchise, which I loved. Covid hit and that job folded. I then transitioned into my current position, where I enjoy my love of video creation and editing. I have developed quite a few of the IFs into, "WHEN do you need that project completed?"

Chapter 23

The Miami Project

After a brief stay at Bellevue, they transferred me to NYU Rusk Rehab at 1st Avenue and 34th Street. It was right next to where the police helicopter had landed on that life-changing day. I had a weekday schedule of rehab, which included physical therapy and occupational therapy. In between classes, they would put us back into our beds for two hours of rest and lunch. While watching the TV, I heard that the son of Nick Buoniconti, Marc, had sustained a spinal cord injury when making a tackle for his Citadel football team. Months later, after my rehab discharge, I heard about a new organization that had formed in Miami.

Jackson Memorial is the main trauma hospital in Miami, where Dr. Barth Green had teamed up with Nick Buoniconti to form the Miami Project to Cure Paralysis. Dr. Green had been trying to launch a center that would treat and push hard for a cure for spinal cord injuries. Now, the doctor had a famous football player in Nick. They quickly launched their first Sports Legends Dinner, which honors sports figures, bringing in much needed donations. They held the first event at the Waldorf Astoria in New York City. It was an enormous success and continues to this day. The dinner/fundraiser moved to The New York Hilton a few years ago. During Covid, the 2020-21 event was conducted virtually. Many millions of dollars have been raised to fight for the cure.

I called "The Project" to inquire about the research programs that they were conducting. I requested an application for the functional electrical stimulation study of the upper body — fitting the criteria, which called for people with cervical injuries. We received the news of my acceptance into the study rather quickly. The study would begin on March 1, 1987.

Getting to Miami required an airplane flight from NYC. Boarding the plane was an experience that I wish on no one. They transferred me from my daily chair to an uncomfortable, straight back, narrow aluminum chair. Once you are at your designated seat, they manhandled me into it. For the duration of the flight, there are no bathroom breaks. I drank a minimal amount of water so that I did not have to be catheterized in flight. So many years after the ADA passage, there are still no bathroom facilities for the disabled. I have taken six flights as a paralyzed man. It's no picnic. Dad had just retired and my mom, who was still working as a nurse, took a leave of absence to afford me participation in the research study. Mom tended to my health needs and dad did the lifting and driving.

The upper extremity study took four months. Fortunately, my second cousin had a condo in Hollywood that he let us use.

Dad & me - Hollywood, FL - 1987

We were grateful to have a place to stay. Three days a week, we would all travel down I-95 for my therapy. The physical therapist concentrated on my wrist flexors. They used sticky pads, similar to the ones used for an EKG, which were placed on my wrist and forearm. The electrical impulse was initiated as I looked at a computer screen and at the signal by the therapist, I focused on moving my wrist in time with the stimulation. I regained some flexion of my wrists, but not enough that was functional.

When the upper body FES (functional electrical stimulation) was ending, I was asked if I would like to stay and continue for a lower extremity FES study that would be conducted on an FES bicycle. Mom received an extension of her leave. They connected the same type of pads with wires to my glutes, hamstrings, and quadriceps. The stimulation mimics the firing of the nerves to the muscles that an able-bodied person has when riding a bicycle.

The study was setup as a one-shot session, meaning that you rode up to fatigue or sometimes you only achieved two minutes. FES and your muscles, working in conjunction, can either result in a brief session or a long session — which is not in your control. Some days I had a quick ride and other

Mom & me - Miami Project - 1987

days a long one. I created an uncomfortable environment for my parents, who lovingly tolerated my anger. I was quick-tempered and unpleasant. I wanted to ride the bike with just the therapist present — I felt I needed to regain some sort of independence. Regrettably, after a few sessions, I requested my parents let me ride the bike without their presence. I know that hurt them. I still feel sad for excluding them. They accepted my decision, went to the nearby office, and helped with mailings of publications to promote the program. To this day, I cannot shake my selfish moment. All I could do was ask for forgiveness.

Since we were in downtown Miami, we took advantage of the surrounding offerings. We did all the touristy things like monkey jungle, parrot jungle, etc. The coolest place we frequented was Biscayne Bay, where my dad would set up a foldable chaise-lounge in the warm water and he and mom would pick me up from my wheelchair and place me in it. The views of Miami from across the bay were fabulous.

Sometimes my father and I would drive aimlessly all-around Broward and Dade county on off days. As a young boy, we would drive around on Sundays back home in Westchester County. I usually knew an area that we never explored. I know he didn't always want to venture out — my dad was an extremely selfless man. I excelled and enjoyed the FES bike, and my carpenter's insurance purchased one for home use. I rode the bike for a short time but had to stop because of multiple recurring tears in my sacral area. We donated the machine to a rehab center in New Jersey.

Although I only gained a small amount of function from my Miami Project stay, I grew more confident in myself and in my abilities.

Overall, it was a rewarding experience. I am still involved with The Project. My parents, many family members and friends give generously to the cause. We have a chapter here in Charleston that holds an annual fundraiser during a Citadel football game. I know that my chances of regaining function again become slimmer as the years go by. I've made peace with that. We are proud of our part toward the cause for a cure. Someday, all paralyzed people will benefit from discoveries made at The Miami Project. Hopefully, one day, a cure for paralysis will be as routine as setting a broken limb.

Me, John, Marc and Susan at Miami Project Fundraisers

Catherine Bell, Leigh & John Stephens, Me   My return to The Miami Project

Chapter 24

New Ride

About halfway through my research study at The Miami Project, my mother asked me if I was interested in learning how to drive. I hadn't thought of it. I knew a quadriplegic in rehab who learned to drive. Pete was a level better off than me. I did not know that there were adaptations available for me to drive. Since I can't transfer by myself, I had to drive from my wheelchair with special accommodations for gas, brake, and steering, along with a lift that would afford me access in and out of the van.

I teamed up with a driving specialist that the project provided and got an idea of what I could do. There were two conversion companies in the Miami area. I received a tip from a fellow research subject on which one to use. They were a small father and son operation. My parents bought a new, stripped-down van, and we met with the technician to hash out exactly what I needed to drive safely. I must admit, it was scary, especially my first drive on I-95. Within a few weeks, I felt confident. They completed the van in February, and I still had my hard neck brace on from a surgery that was performed in January. The doctor removed some bone fragments from my neck that were close to my spinal cord. The procedure was called a post anterior decompression. There was a possibility of more damage if these fragments were not removed. Before I was closed up, a piece of bone was harvested from my left hip and a fusion of my fourth, fifth and sixth cervical vertebrae was performed.

I now had a lot more freedom with the van. I drove it up from Hollywood, FLA to Yonkers, NY. We made a stop at the Antietam Battlefield in the morning and an afternoon visit to Gettysburg. From there, after an overnight stay in a hotel, I drove straight home from York, PA.

I-95, to the motherland - 1988

Spring had sprung in New York, and I cruised to a few of my favorite places. Most of my friends had moved on. There were a few friends that I still had from my previous life, and I cherished them.

Two weeks before my sister Pat's wedding, me and two of my neighborhood friends ate at the famous Greasy Nick's hamburger and seafood joint. On the way back home, as I was attempting to negotiate an incline on Kings Highway, my chair broke loose from its lock-down. I was in a manual chair, my hand positioned in a tri-pin assembly that accelerated by pulling back on its pole. As my wheelchair became dislodged, my hand was still connected to the acceleration, tri-pin/pole assembly. I was rolling back, which made the van go faster. I was finally released from the assembly and was positioned in the middle of my van that was heading toward a parking structure. That peculiar, familiar state of mind of slow motion right before impact was with me once more.

The van crashed into a structural I-beam of an office building's ground level parking lot at approximately twenty mph. It launched me forward toward the driving station where a one foot long, billet aluminum steering wheel extension was waiting for me. Fortunately, my chair veered to the left and this hunk of aluminum did not impale me at my mid-section. That would have been internal destruction.

First accessible ride - 1988

My right thigh took the brunt from the beast, leaving me with a compound fracture of the right femur. Jack, who was riding shotgun, made contact with the windshield, just as I did. JJ, who was lounging on the back bench seat, took a flight to the front. He sustained no injuries. I was very lucky that afternoon. I had just passed a gas station on my left before going up the incline. What a horror show that would have been if the van collided with the gas pumps. I cringe to this day, thinking about that scenario. EMS was on the scene quickly; I had a concussion from the windshield impact and was unsuccessfully trying to get the side door open with my controls. The door had been jammed shut. They ended up taking me out through the back doors after removal of the bench seat. My cervical fusion a few months prior strengthened my spine, saving me from another broken neck.

I was in traction for a few weeks at New Rochelle Hospital to allow for my wound to heal a bit before they set my femur and inserted two titanium rods. Thank God we all survived that one. I wondered how the heck my wheelchair became dislodged from its lock-down. I questioned myself, did I do something wrong? My sister Michele hired a crash expert who discovered the weld that secured my wheelchair to the van's lock-down system was defective and had broken free. I was relieved knowing that I did nothing incorrectly. I was without independent transportation for nearly a year as the insurance settlement and the build of a new van in New Jersey were completed.

My new van had a drop-down elevator, six inches deep. I even incorporated a manual lock on the side of my chair, along with an electric e-z lock. Triple security. I would not allow that incident to repeat.

Second Van - 1989

My second van had its odometer spun. That van took me all around the New York tri-state area, the hills of the Blue Ridge Parkway, then to our new home in South Carolina. I drove one more van, then my health took a nosedive, and I thought it was best for my safety and for the safety of others to give up driving. Now, I am a passenger in my latest van, annoying my family as the world's best backseat driver.

Chapter 25

Lee

It was the summer of 1991 when I received a phone call from my oldest brother, Doug. "Jim, I have some interesting news about an organization that just formed down here, west of Philly." At the time, I was still living in my childhood home in Yonkers, NY. I was six years post SCI injury and a few years away from moving down to South Carolina. There was a write-up in his local paper announcing the beginning of a service dog organization called "Canine Partners for Life." He thought I may benefit with the assistance of a trained service dog. I thought it was a wonderful idea. I contacted CPL, and they sent me an application asking about myself and what expectations I had regarding a service dog. My sheet included my inability to pick up dropped objects, such as my writing/eating brace, fork, towel, and things of that sort. Darlene Sullivan, the Founder/Director, called me and said that I would be a perfect candidate for a service dog. She also informed me that her certified dogs could also assist in opening a department store door and pay cashiers. She set a date and my brother Bill took a trip with me and our parents to Cochranville, Pennsylvania.

Cochranville, PA - 1992

Darlene matched me with a black lab named Butchie. He was halfway through his training and would be ready by the Fall of 1991. As soon as I deployed my lift, Butchie jumped right into the van. He was raring to go! We visited the rest of the afternoon, gave him some love, and I drove back home with my family. Darlene sent a few progress reports, along with a book, which had tips on lots of fundamentals regarding care and first-time owner kind of stuff. Shortly after receiving the book, I got a call from Darlene. She sounded sad. "Jim, I have bad news for you. Yesterday, we had to put Butchie down. He was having episodes of falling and uneasiness on his feet. It was determined by the vet that he had a neurological disease." It saddened me to hear this news. I felt bad, but I honestly could not say that I was heartbroken. We met for a moment, and our pairing wasn't meant to be.

Shortly after this news, Darlene informed me of a second dog that she thought would be a good fit. We headed back down to Cochranville to see the new candidate. Well, my mini disaster had just begun. Before I had entered the large barn, where the dogs were being housed, Darlene told me that her name was Heather. Jeez, I mumbled under my breath. The dog had the same name as a past, on-and-off girl-friend. How the heck am I going to call this innocent animal one hundred times a day, and not constantly be reminded of her? Upon entering the barn to meet Heather, I observed her jumping vertically, like a circus animal. Whoa, strike two! Darlene let her out, and she came over for a greet. She was a beautiful dog, but large for me to handle. I don't know if Darlene was sensing a mixture of my concern and fear, but she shut it down right then. She was an excellent trainer, and she knew Heather had potential, but was just not a good match for me. I was relieved. Back up to NY to wait for the perfect match.

After my return home, I developed a significant pressure sore in my tailbone area. Receiving a dog was put on hold until the Spring of 1992. During my healing process, Darlene received a call from the Delaware SPCA. "Hey, we have a smart one here for you. He was adopted out yesterday, and this morning they tied him to a tree on our property." We never found out the reason that adoption was an unsuitable match between the local SPCA and the recipient. Thank God for that! The names of the service dogs are not in the recipient's control. I've heard a few names, usually given to the dog by a family puppy home, when it is waiting to be trained. In this instance, there was no family involved. They housed this dog that I was hopefully going to receive with Darlene's mother and father. When I heard his name, I breathed a sigh of relief. My boy, my son, was named Lee.

My boy Lee - 1993

Technically, he was named Lion Lee, taking on the name of the local Lions Club, who sponsored his training. The only time I referred to Lee as Lion Lee was during training at a diner, when co-incidentally, the Lion's Club was having a breakfast meeting. I introduced myself and Lion Lee to the members. "Where are you from, shouted a member?" "Yonkers,

NY, I replied." "Ah, I've been to Yonkers a few times on business." I didn't ask where, I probably should have. Darlene and I thanked them for their sponsorship and off we went. There were two others in my group. Fred, who had multiple sclerosis, and Dave, who had muscular dystrophy. My mother and I made the trip to Christiana, Delaware. Mom stayed in the hotel room during the day, and I drove fifteen miles up into Pennsylvania for daily training. Darlene preferred we keep it just recipients and service dogs for training and outings. Looking back, I should have spoken up and told Darlene that there was going to be an exception, but I didn't, another regret to add to my life's worth.

My poor mom had two choices during the day, other than staying in the hotel and reading. It was either a visit to Toys-R-Us or a Chi Chi's restaurant, both within walking distance. That was it, unless she wanted to walk through some brush to I-95 and watch traffic whiz by. The training lasted three weeks. Generally, after the first week, your service dog stays with you for the duration of your training in the hotel room. Fortunately, all of us bonded so well with our dogs, they stayed with us after just three days. Lee rarely left my side, except for surgeries that both of us had in the future. Initially, my schedule back home did not allow for a full day up in the chair. My mom walked Lee in the morning before she boarded the commuter train down to Harlem, where she worked as a nurse. I don't know how she managed that half-mile walk up the boulevard and still made it to the train on time. She was my rock then and now.

Lee was a handsome border collie mix with beautiful eyes. When I received him, they estimated his age to be about one and a half years. We would now embark, pun intended, on our new lives together as a team. First order of business when we got back home was to get out into the world and run through some skills. We went out shopping and ran through the "open up the heavy mall door maneuver." This involved a few skills that had to be done precisely. Lee wore a leather harness crafted by an Amish leather master, and we incorporated a strap with a painter's hook. I would grab the strap with the hook and connect it to the door, unhook Lee's leash, then I would give him the command to come towards me. He would get the door open, then I would give the stay command as I moved toward the door to block it open with my wheelchair.

Mom & Lee - Yonkers, NY - 1993

Unhook the strap from the door handle and connect it to Lee's harness. Then I told him to come around and gave him a sit-stay command. After determining that door was safe, I gave a go-through command, and another sit-stay, then I went through the door. Now we were in the foyer, and need to go through another set of doors, starting the entire process over again. He was a strong, healthy boy, weighing in at forty-five lbs. I saw the strain on his body and opted not to continue opening the heavy department store doors. I loved him and I could not put him through any more of these exercises. He had plenty of other things to help me with, as well as being my constant companion and advisor.

We worked well as a team and we began helping at my old elementary school, reading with students on a one-on-one basis. I did this volunteer work with three children for two years. It was a rewarding experience, and the children liked both of us, Lee, a bit more! It wasn't long after receiving Lee that we moved near Charleston, SC. After some serious thought, I decided to study at college, choosing commercial graphics. None of these tasks would have been accomplished without my ever-present, loving mother, father, and family. I must admit, I know Lee loved me, but his Grammy did not give him the constant commands, and she slipped him some extra treats. We kept up the training that was required by Canine Partners for Life. I would do verbal and silent arm commands for sit, down, stay, heel, as well as give, and take, keeping Lee and myself fine-tuned.

Lee's veterinarian, who conveniently practiced close to our home, nominated him in the 1999 SCAV Hall of Fame - Professional Service Dog Division. Dr. George, I, sister Michele, and others submitted stories about our life together. We traveled up to Myrtle Beach, where we enjoyed two days at a high-rise resort on the beach.

Myrtle Beach, SC - 1999

At the closing beachfront BBQ dinner, Lee was awarded the First Place Winner. They presented him with a plaque, which I accepted on his behalf. When the MC asked, "where shall I place the ribbon?" I told him to hold it out and I'll command Lee to take it. Lee sauntered away from the presentation area with his blue ribbon in his mouth, back to my side. That was an enjoyable experience, which had a nice writeup in the paper.

140

The CPL program required a visit after one year. I was in the area, as my brother was getting married in PA, close to Darlene's parents' home. She was by the book, and I knew that as a team, we had to be a cohesive unit to pass inspection. We did and continued to, every other year, for ten years. Being down south meant that I was outside of the two hundred fifty-mile zone and was not required to go to Cochranville for our recertification. Darlene had a trainer contact in Savannah, where we met for two recertifications. Our final two were done by video, which had to be continuous with no editing. After ten years together, Lee could no longer jump up into the van, which was a requirement. They decertified him as a service dog. He performed his job with precision and joy and was retired, staying at home with our family.

The last year of his life, Lee developed sicknesses and one time had to be kept overnight at the vet. He was a very friendly boy, and I gave him a lot of freedom to interact with people. Some recipients were much more rigid than I was. He was my boy, and I wanted him to be happy. He knew his job well — we went everywhere; we were inseparable. I loved him and he loved me, along with the rest of our family. I knew it was his time, but I couldn't let go. I couldn't even make the call. He was suffering. My mother intervened and made the call to the vet. It was a duty that I should have done weeks prior. It was such a hard decision — I was selfish and could not let him go. I knew it was for the best. My brother-in-law, Doug, placed Lee into the back of our Volvo wagon and drove him to the top of the street as I followed in my wheelchair.

Lee was brought in and placed on the exam table. The doctor walked me through the process. This was the hardest moment of my life. My eyes never left his; he was still alive, then the doctor quietly told me he would be passing shortly. I saw his eye go from movement to a complete stop. I've never been so heartbroken. It has been many years and I'm crying my eyes out as I write this passage. The doctor left the room to give us privacy. I stayed with Lee for a while, then gave him my last stroke on his beautiful, long black hair. Leaving that room was difficult. For weeks afterwards, I passed by the door that we both went through on that last day.

His ashes are in my closet, on the shelf, and when I am called, we will be as one with each other. Our earthly remains will be scattered together at the Pitt Street Bridge, into the waters of Charleston Harbor, where my dad's ashes are. We had a beautiful life together — Lee enriched mine, as well as my family. We will meet on that rainbow bridge, along with my dad, who will stand tall without his wheelchair. Lee, dad, and my departed family will be united again, and we will play and do all the earthly things together once more.

Chapter 26

The Move

Dad and mom had retired, and it was time for a reassessment of our future. We were being enticed to the south by my sister Pat, who had just built a home with her husband, Victor, in Mt. Pleasant, SC. We were receiving reports of fantastic weather and the beauty that surrounded their new home. Pat found us a brand-new apartment, which was across the harbor from Charleston. The decision was made, and the family home was put up for sale. We gathered our essentials and moved the rest of our possessions into storage. It was time. We still had family in the area, but there were the cold winters to deal with and the summer heat without air conditioning. During those heat waves, my dad would fill a wide bucket of cold water with ice for me to soak my feet in.

The only home that I ever knew was in Yonkers, NY. A three-story Dutch Colonial, built in 1917. I always got a kick out of knowing that the Bolshevik Revolution coincided with our family home being built. Full disclosure — my Grandparents, dad and his two brothers moved there in the summer of 1934. My bedroom on the third floor was no longer accessible. We had a large side room on the first floor that was cleared out to make space for my bed and new equipment. Beautiful, mature plantings surrounded the home. The backyard forsythia bloomed a vibrant yellow in the early spring. Although hard to wheel on, the gravel driveway was elegant and complemented the beautifully landscaped rhododendron and azaleas that framed our home. The outside surely had its beauty, as did the inside. My favorite was the fireplace hearth whereas a child I would always ask dad if we could get a fire going. He never denied me that pleasure. If a fire was going to get started, I needed to gather the wood, which was in the back right corner of the property. We had a mother lode of good burning maple and ash from trimmings over the years. I loved sitting cross-legged on the floor, enjoying the glow. The next morning, I would open the small trap door and funnel the ashes into the shaft that collected in the furnace room wall.

Bradford Blvd - Yonkers, NY

In my seventh year of paralysis, living in the side sunroom, dad had his first leg amputation, below the knee. His other leg was not faring well and making his way up to the second-floor bedroom had become too difficult. For a while, we bunked together in the same room. Eventually, he moved his bed into the dining room. I watched TV well into the wee hours. It was the five of us in this large house that was being underutilized and not serving our purposes any longer. I knew I was mentally prepared to leave, as were my folks. My dad had lived in this home since 1934, with an eleven-year absence when my parents raised our family in an apartment in Mount Vernon, NY. My fraternal grandmother died in 1963 and my grandfather occupied the big old house. Pop-Pop moved to Chicago, and we all moved into his house. He eventually settled in Bal Harbor, Florida.

We did our visits to all the places that we enjoyed over the years and when the day came to finally shove off to South Carolina; I was not sad one bit. I had made peace with leaving my childhood home. There was nothing left there for me. My friends had all begun their next chapters many years before. My consistent neighborhood friend, "Crazy JJ" was still around. To hear JJ speak is comparable to listening to a downpour of words. Many a night, when there was a snowfall, he would drive his snowmobile through the streets for hours. I tracked his location by his open exhaust. He was there for me when I needed him. I hear from him every couple of years with news of who is still alive. During this semi-dark time in my life, I did harbor ill feelings toward the many people that I knew who no longer came around or even phoned. It hurt, and it took time for me to get over it. I had to start anew, reinvent myself in some fashion. South Carolina was where my personal phoenix rose from the ash heap that I was mired in.

We traveled convoy style. My oldest sister Michele and father drove the Dodge Dynasty, as I maintained 55 mph in the right lane, occasionally topping out at 60. My father and sister would hold up notes at the window, telling me to "gun it." It was 1995 and the speed limit was 65 mph. I was a 55 mph driver when I was able-bodied, so why change now? It took us two days to arrive. Dad, mom, grandmother, me, and my service dog Lee moved into the freshly built apartment that Pat secured for us. Dad and I scouted the town for a building lot where we would eventually build our forever home. Our primary aim was to find a lot that was at least 100 ft by 100 ft, since it was to be a one floor home except for a room over the garage. After an exhaustive search of nearly every street in town, we came across a lot on a long dead-end road. Finally, a regular old road. Most neighborhoods in the town were subdivisions which carried regime fees and petty restrictions. I made a call to the realtor to inquire about the price. I made an offer, and it was accepted, which was exhilarating.

Mom found a plan for a house that she liked and shared it with us. We weren't quite ready to build, so we studied the floor plan and saw where we would like changes. Along came hurricane season, and we found ourselves in our first evacuation. We made camp at a motel seventy-five miles away. Eating dinner that night, mom found a Southern Living magazine with a plan for a house. This plan was far superior to our current one. That evacuation had a happy ending! I was in my first year at college and would go to the building site after class regularly. The contractor built a makeshift ramp that allowed me to check on the framing that was underway. The hurricane building codes had been improved substantially after the debacle of Hurricane Hugo that hit Charleston in 1989, and Andrew, which tore apart Homestead, FLA in 1992. Every framing member was strengthened with metal strapping.

Before we made the move, hurricanes were always in the back of my mind. I calmed myself, knowing that in SC, we had escape routes in two different directions, as opposed to the folks in FLA who could only go north. Our street had access to a frontage road that ran the length of the state road. My folks and I would travel to stores, the hospital and across to the Old Village, all on the frontage road. A streetlight and a fire hydrant on our front corners were a bonus. We had and have good neighbors and live peacefully on our quiet street in the bustling "town" of Mount Pleasant. We have lost dad, Nanny, and Lee but fortunately mom and my five siblings are still alive.

Chapter 27

Susquehanna

Susquehanna — just saying the word makes me smile. I first heard this delightful word as a boy, perched in front of the TV, watching an afternoon Abbott & Costello routine. Their Susquehanna Hat Company skit still cracks me up today. A trip to Cooperstown, NY, to visit the Major League Baseball Hall of Fame situated me and family at Otsego Lake — the headwaters of the mighty Susquehanna River. It was 1990, and we weren't long for Yonkers.

I booked two rooms a stone's throw from the lakefront marina, one block from the baseball mecca. My dad, me, sister Mary Ellen and brother Doug headed up on my last opportunity to visit the hall. The 190-mile trip upstate was a half day drive. Dad was my navigator — a human GPS, way before the term was in popular use. He could not only read a map well, he also folded the darn thing correctly! He set the route, north up I-87 to Albany, then onto US-20 to NY-80, where we entered Cooperstown at the southern tip of Otsego Lake.

After check-in, we hit the hall, taking in the plaques of our favorites and the seemingly endless number of displays. On the second floor, every team had an individual locker display of their current uniforms, including spikes and assorted bats. We made the obligatory stop at the Cubs locker

Dad, Doug & me - Cooperstown, NY - 1992

and the Babe Ruth locker, which was prominently displayed away from the modern clubs. Another highlight was seeing the gray road uniform of Willie Mays — with its black on orange, arched, "SAN FRANCISCO" letters, tight across the upper chest.

Dad played ball for the Tuckahoe Robins in the Hudson Valley League. His thumb, which was not set correctly, was a reminder of his playing days at the Tuckahoe Oval, with its beautiful outfield views of the Bronx River. In his heyday, baseball was king, with college football a close second.

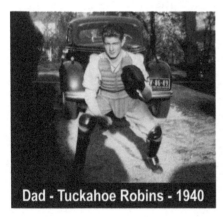

Dad - Tuckahoe Robins - 1940

Dad was born in Chicago, with moves to Omaha, Indianapolis, Milwaukee, and Philadelphia, before finally settling in Yonkers, NY at age nine. He fervently followed his beloved Cubbies throughout his life. His favorite players were fellow catcher Gabby Hartnett and Ernie Banks, "Mr. Cub." He was a power hitting shortstop/first baseman, hitting 512 home runs.

Ernie was also known for his many tales of the origin of his "let's play two" proclamation.

In his teen and early adult years, dad had easy access to Cubs games when they came to town to play the New York Giants at the Polo Grounds. I willingly boarded that heartache train and rode out the agony, attending Met games when the Cubs came to Big Shea. The Cubs consistently broke our hearts, especially when they tanked their first place run in 1969. When a black cat crossed Ron Santo's path outside of the on-deck circle at Shea, then stared down the team in the dugout, their fate was sealed. The Metropolitan Baseball Club put together a late season surge and continued on to beat the Baltimore Orioles for their first World Series title.

The day finally arrived for us Cub fans in the 2016 World Series, with a three-game comeback against the Cleveland Indians.

Wrigley Field - 2016

Sadly, my dad and Ernie were no longer with us to see the Cubs win the big one. We were all glued to the TV, witnessing the miracle. Thank you, dad, for bringing me into the fold. The multiple years of disappointment were well worth it — we were together.

Cubs management permitted fans to write messages with chalk on the brick wall that surrounds Wrigley Field. Brother Doug's friend, Bob, a Chicago resident, found a spot on the dark, weathered mortar where he honored our father. Thank you, Bob, for thinking about our dad!

Visiting Cooperstown, with the additional gift of seeing the headwaters of the Susquehanna, was the appetizer in my discovery of the river. During training in the spring of 1992, with my service dog Lee, at Cochranville, Pennsylvania, mom, and I took a Saturday day trip to an outlet in Maryland. We arrived at the freshly built mini complex, did some shopping, and had lunch. Driving across US-40, I had my second view of the Susquehanna. Some 440 miles from its headwaters, we were at its terminus, where the river released its massive flow to the head of the Chesapeake Bay. So much beauty in between that I can only glean through photos.

After crossing the two-mile bridge, we entered the town of Havre De Grace, Maryland. We drove around town and came across two women at a quiet intersection. We chatted a bit and upon leaving, I asked, "what's a must-see in your town?" They proudly replied, "you're in the decoy capital of the world!" My puzzled look gave me away. "You know, ducks and geese? We have a museum here." I thanked them, skipped the museum, and drove back to our motel with no regrets. I already reaped my reward — my first and only headwaters to head.

Havre De Grace has an Otsego Street, acknowledging the source of the grand river. Well done.

Chapter 28

College

It was 9:50am as I sat in my van with my service dog, Lee. I found a parking spot close to the building, but the process of unloading both myself and Lee soaked us. We made it to the foyer of the building. Lee gave his body a shake. He removed a large amount of the water from his fur, and I wiped his head as best I could. I'm drenched. I rubbed my hand across my head and removed some water. Onward we went to English Composition 101. When we arrived at my class, I luckily found a spot in the first row by the door. The room was full, and everyone received the waft of my wet pup. I thought that the first day would be a breeze, filled with introductions and going over the syllabus. Wrong. The instructor told us to write a short story about ourselves. OK, I got to work, still dripping. Lee seemed comfortable by my side and had the attention of a pleasant woman to my left.

The campus at Trident Technical College was exactly fifteen miles from my home. The ride was just long enough for me to quiz myself before tests. Generally, I took two to three classes per semester — my field of study was commercial graphics. A month prior to my first class, I had to physically register on the main campus. It was

1997 and most colleges were doing online registration. Tech still did it the old-fashioned way and required us to show up at the registrar's building. If you wanted a particular class that was in high demand, you had to show up early. Doors opened at 8am, which meant that I had to be in line outside the building at 5am, weather be damned.

The first time I went through this obsolete exercise, there were already ten students in line at 5am. For me to get up and ready required a 4am wake up. My poor mother had to endure this bullshit for the three years that it took for me to earn my associate's degree. When registering, I kept Lee at home with mom and dad. He didn't sign up for this. College was my only way of gaining knowledge for a career in graphics and the computer field. In one of my classes, we were required to separate colors using amberlith. It was an extinct procedure, but the instructors made us go through it to gain the knowledge and be strained as they were. By this time, computers had taken over the processes of color separation required by the printing industry. In this class, I cut over fifty sheets. I could handle the X-Acto knife in my brace and cut the artwork. I needed assistance from my mom to peel the waste from the base sheet. Then each sheet of amberlith had to be layered on top of each other with the Pantone color code listed. Finally, a cover sheet with your name was written on the back. It was a challenge, but I wanted to accomplish what they assigned the rest of my classmates. I made a sweet setup in my room that included an adjustable table to work on color separations and other precision work.

In my pre-injury days, a college campus was the last place that you would find me, with the exception of visiting a friend. Back then, I had other priorities and interests. Life threw me a curveball, and I had to travel another path. I excelled in class, enjoyed collaborating with my classmates, and meeting deadlines. I loved the challenge of creating media pieces on the computer and in the darkroom. It was a real-life preparation for my future employment. I went from not knowing how to turn on a computer to being proficient by the time that I graduated. There were classes that were sheer drudgery, math being the main one. College algebra and probability and statistics were my biggest challenges. I had to take two non-credit math classes to be eligible for algebra class. That chewed up valuable time. I loved the computer, photography, and art classes, along with the rest of my core subjects.

I was permitted to join my classmates at the North Charleston Coliseum for spring commencement, even though I had two more classes to complete in the summer. That was a standard that they afforded all students. When lining up to march onto the floor, I was approached by one of my art instructors, who placed a silver medal around my neck. I asked Ms. Smith what this was for. She replied, "this is your medal, your Magna Cum Laude." I did not expect it. I knew my GPA was 3.8, but a medal? Cool! I was strictly there to get an education, but this was nice. Now, in order to keep that medal, I had to pass my final two classes. One was an advertising art class. That one I was confident I would ace. The other class was the dreaded probability and statistics, where I had to earn no less than a B. A tall order.

I studied hard during the week and on weekends. By the time the class was ending, it had dwindled from twenty-five students to ten. Lots dropped out, just as they did during my public speaking class. Bring on the final exam! I needed an 82 on this exam to reach that elusive B. The instructor informed us he would grade our exams if we wished to stay and wait after everyone had completed theirs. I opted to stay. It was make-or-break time. He handed my exam back with an 85 circled on top! That was a darn pleasant moment. I remember driving out of the south end of campus and screaming that "Elvis has left the building!" My hard work had been rewarded.

Between my second and third year at Tech, the head of the department asked if I would like to take a position as an intern in a newly formed business incubator in downtown Charleston, across from Marion Square. My position was graphics, working with a student from The Citadel, who was studying computer science, and a student from the College of Charleston, who was studying journalism. Together, we built a website for the incubator that housed a dozen future entrepreneurs. We also assisted them with any of their needs. This job coincided with my school workload. I drove downtown three days a week to work from nine to two. It was a paying internship, funded by a grant from NOAA. The internship had a one hour paid lunch — a federal government bonus. Most days I brown bagged it and ate a few blocks away at the Gaillard Auditorium gardens, usually having a sandwich and Lee would eat his big milk bone. Some days we visited the Dog Pound for hot dogs. We had a lot of time, so we strolled around the Ansonboro district and ventured down to the Charleston City Market regularly. That internship was a rewarding experience, where I met a lot of interesting people from around the country.

At my commencement, our guest speaker was Daniel Ruettiger, the actual Rudy guy from the movie. He was fabulous, and I thought it was quite cool, being that his movie was one of my favorites. School ended, and I needed to find a job. I checked the boards on campus where jobs were posted and found one a few blocks from my house. I did not know that All American Awards was doing business so close. I phoned the owner and inquired about their opening — they needed someone with a graphic background to create and layout award pieces. He hired me immediately after showing him my book. Once my layouts were completed, they were sent to another employee to be sandblasted, sublimated or lasered onto glass, acrylic, wood, or metal. I worked there for ten years. The commute was ideal, except for the danger of driving in the bike lane, where cars make it their own. I was without a job for a few years and then was employed by a cruise franchise, where I worked for seven years in social media. I am presently working at a newly formed company, using my video creation and editing skills.

Chapter 29

Mustang to Whiskey

After being home for a while, I overheard that a friend of my sister Pat had involved herself in a voluntary program that taught English as a second language. I asked a few questions and was told that the local library had weekly meetings where training was given on how to teach those that were beginners with English. We met for three hours, once a week. At the time, I was not driving — sister Ellie arrived home from work at 4pm, transferred me into her car, and drove to the library for my 5pm training.

They gave us the basics in four meetings and assigned us students. I met my student in the children's section of the Grinton I. Will library branch. On our first encounter, his wife, who spoke English well, accompanied him. It was downhill from there; I was stood up twice. There was no other student on a waiting list to take his place. To continue on in this program, I would have to wait until the next session in six months.

Out of the blue, I had an idea. I went up to my old elementary school, P.S. 28, spoke to the principal, asking if they needed anyone who could help the children in any way — whether it be reading or speaking with the students. Dr. Roosevelt was very warm to my idea and assigned me to the teacher, who would coordinate students. She asked me what year I graduated from P.S. 28, and she was excited when I told her. "Did you have Mrs. Charette? She is my best friend." Oh, my, what a coincidence, she was my sixth-grade teacher. We hated her. She was called the "Canadian" or "the screamer." My preference was the full, formal, "Canadian screamer." She was an intimidating teacher. I replied, "she was a gem."

My first student was a third grader, who was very timid. I believe it may have been her unfamiliarity with my wheelchair. She was under my reading guidance for a month, then school went into summer recess. In the fall, I began again, assigned with a fourth-grade boy. It was surreal to be in the hallways and classrooms from so many years ago. Everything was tiny. The reading lab teacher asked the fourth-grade boy if he would mind helping me take off my chest strap and coat and put my coat and strap back on when we were done. He agreed, and I gave him permission to pet and play with Lee, my service dog. We got along well. He was eager to read to me and Lee. Hopefully, he continued to thrive.

P.S. 28 was only three blocks from home. At the time that I volunteered there, especially in bad weather, required safety incorporated into my travels. We were years before the cell phone and the only communication, other than a beeper, was the CB radio. I owned a set. Dad and I needed "handles." They came to me in an instant — I was Mustang, and dad was Whiskey. We communicated through the radio halfway to my three-block trip to school. I would call out, "Mustang to Whiskey - Mustang to Whiskey, come in Whiskey" and my dad would interrupt his constitutional of reading the paper from cover to cover to take my call out. "Mustang, you have Whiskey - over." "I'm halfway, Whiskey, and will call upon arrival - over." We got a kick out of it. If I got stuck on the road without communication, I was screwed. So far, in my thirty-seven years of rambling around in my wheelchair travel machine, I've only had one incident. I rode home from that same school, once, with a nail puncture — on rubber and rim. Now I only ride on solid tires.

My third student seemed older; I was later informed by a teacher that they had indeed left him back two years. I felt for the child. He seemed uncomfortable around his smaller, less mature classmates. I thought I knew the ins and outs of this school, but there was an unknown storage room just past the stage entrance that we used for our reading lab. After introductions, my student began with inappropriate questions regarding my girlfriend status. I stopped him dead in his tracks and explained that we were here for me to listen to him read and explain the meaning and use of any unfamiliar words, nothing more. He made another attempt, this time telling me about his multiple girlfriends. Okay, stop, we're done for today. I found my reading lab teacher, explained what happened and please call me if another student was ready to learn. I had no more children, and a term break was close.

We were on the verge of a move by the start of school, after Labor Day. My interactions with two of the three students were joyous and memorable. It was a learning experience for me and hopefully for the children, especially the fourth-grade boy who was enthusiastic about learning, reading and Lee. I believe I gave a bit of good to a few children.

Chapter 30

Floyd

"Strawberry Snoballs is all they have left," shouted my sister Pat as she exited the truck stop store. "Screw that crap," I yelled back. The revolting smell of diesel exhaust was wafting through the parking lot and the light rain that had just begun was a welcome relief on my shirtless body. We were in our tenth hour of evacuation from Charleston. I rolled over to a trucker and asked what his plan was. "I'm staying put until this traffic thins out." Now, that's going to work for him, being that he has a spot behind the wheel where he can sleep. I'm in a family convoy that includes my sister, her husband, their three children, my father, and my grandmother in their minivan. I'm driving my van with my mother and service dog Lee. We still had the option of heading back home. The wind speed still allowed us passage over the two bridges to get back to Mount Pleasant. It was not advisable to attempt a passage at sustained winds of forty mph. We huddled together and decided to push on with the masses towards shelter from this oncoming massive storm. Floyd was deceptive, and it gave folks a scare because of its size, initial wind speed and unpredictable movement. Not that we were newbies in 1999 — we had been here for six years and did an evacuation three years prior. Traffic on our first evacuation was considerably lighter because of the smaller population.

Back we went to I-26, headed west towards I-95. In these ten hours, we traveled a mere sixty miles, with twenty more to go to reach Orangeburg, South Carolina, and search for a hotel with two rooms. Traffic was at a standstill as we reentered the snail pace of I-26. At this point, I was beyond exhausted. The heat of the day had dissipated, but I had no energy left in the tank and was close to my breaking point. I was the only one who could operate my modified van. Not wanting to continuously shift from park to drive and risk burning out my electric gear shift, I leaned on to the brake with my left hand and torso. I just needed to close my eyes. Mom would tell me when the traffic started to move again. When nature called, she catheterized me from my driving position. Folks were walking off the highway toward the wooded areas to relieve themselves — there was no road rage. Thousands of us were experiencing the same desperation together. The only vehicles that were trucking by were the prison buses that were evacuating in the breakdown lane. We envied them. I made many calls to the state police, asking when the governor was going to reverse the eastbound lane to Charleston and allow all traffic to head westbound. That never happened. Governor Hodges didn't see a second term. We finally made it to the junction of I-26 and I-95, which was at a complete standstill. Everyone from Florida and Georgia was evacuating, too.

Hello Orangeburg! An eighty-mile drive that would normally take under two hours took us thirteen. When we arrived at the local streets, my brother-in-law hopped out and inquired about vacancies at a half dozen motels with no luck. We were at our wit's end. I could go no further. A hotel manager mentioned that the Orangeburg Regional Medical Center had a special needs shelter. I qualified, along with my mom, who was my direct caregiver, my grandmother, and Lee. My dad, brother-in-law, sister, nieces and nephew were offered to stay one night at the shelter since it would not be filled until the next night. They declined and headed to Asheville, North Carolina, to stay at The Grove Park Inn, where Victor once worked. Pat, Victor, and family had lived in Asheville for a few years prior to their move to the lowcountry.

We settled in a far corner of the massive shelter in a bottom wing of the medical center. They had beds and hot meals for all of us. My mom got busy. She ingeniously erected a walled-off section for us with movable five foot partitions. My head hitting that pillow was a beautiful thing. The nurses and staff told us that night two was going to be a lot different. The room that was so large when we first got there seemed small by noon the next day. There had to be close to three hundred people. Ventilators were audible across the room as the evacuees from the lowcountry met the midlands. The storm came in on the second night and our only fear was tornadoes that usually form on the outer edge of hurricanes. We were in a sturdy building, but it was no match for a tornado. There were none. That next morning, we awoke at 6am and were on the road by 6:45. I boogied home with hardly a vehicle in sight — I literally was, "King of the Road."

When we arrived at the top of our street, I slowed the van and told my mom to be prepared for potential damage to the roof and trees. Halfway down our long, dead-end street, I saw a sign staked into our neighbor's corner road. I stopped and read the message that Dave had posted. "Homeowners only, all others will be shot." He was one of three people on our street that rode out the storm. Landfall skirted past us. Floyd was downgraded to a category two with steady winds of seventy-five mph and gusts of one hundred mph. Our neighbors had experienced Hugo, which was a category four, back in 1989, with landfall winds of one hundred thirty-eight mph. Our house was spared from any damage. We lost a weeping willow tree, which was expected. Our crawl space access door that had a top lever, which was difficult to open, was found in my neighbor's yard. Hurricanes are tricky beasts. There is always the big decision, should we stay, or should we go? If life had do-overs, we would not have fled from hurricane Floyd. The real problem was finding shelter. There are not enough hotels and motels to accommodate that many evacuees. We have a sturdy home, and if it's a category four or less, we will stay. Our property is seventeen feet above sea level and far enough from the ocean and creeks. Hurricanes are part of living in the lowcountry.

Chapter 31

Seis Gatos

The OG was Oreo, named for his black and white markings. He was an indoor/outdoor, streetwise boy, who had reign over a two-block area, with no actual competition to interrupt his daily rounds. He had one glaring defensive fault. When he was in rest mode — which was about 90% of the time — he faced the house, tucked in between its lush plantings, butt exposed.

Oreo

If he had a nemesis, it would have been lights out. I enjoyed playing safari with him. He was quick, with good moves, and had many hiding spots. He slept with my parents, who doted on the ever-purring, kneading boy. Dad would heat up his Fancy Feast breakfast on the gas stove and mom treated him with boiled chicken livers. He strode about his territory with confidence and lived a long, loved life. We moved down south and adopted our neighbor's cat. Rico was nonverbal, he never purred, not even a meow, just the occasional hiss. He was a lone assassin with one aim — to hunt and kill moles. On our front porch, where I have a 180-degree view of the front and side yard, lived his subterranean prey. I was in my morning routine of vitamin D absorption, my chair tilted back, as he dashed by me with two screeching mole pups in his mouth. They were consumed in less than one minute. He became the alpha male, after dethroning Tiger in his simple, effective style. Rico took full advantage of the high ground, as if he was militarily trained. He attacked with a running leap onto Tiger and a swirling fight ensued. After a brief tussle, Rico's reign had begun. He ruled his little kingdom well.

Rico - AKA Rick

Rico was the second inhabitant of the big porch. Tiger Woods, who I named for his stripes, was the first feral cat at our house. He was discovered when my mom noticed the rocking chair was swaying back and forth. Tiger had made the chair his own. He tore the seat and back apart, using it as a scratching post. The chair was not long for the porch and was in the dump down the street in short order. We let him stay or, should I say, he let us stay. Then Vinny appeared. A smaller cat, all gray with one ear injured, lying flat. He appeared to be feral. A modern hybrid of the traditional, unapproachable feral. Seeing his damaged ear, I named him Vincent Van Gogh, Vinny, for short. Rico challenged Vinny in his proven maneuver. He dove off the porch and landed on Vinny in my presence. There was no fight, just Vinny looking at Rico in puzzlement. It was most likely an introduction for the new kid in Rico's kingdom.

Vinny

When Vinny would follow, Rico would turn around and give a hiss. Vinny was looking for a mentor and Rico wanted nothing to do with him. Vinny learned by watching the master. He added skills to his craft in ways that Rico could never imagine. From the big porch, "I see you Vinny, let go of that snake." He was in the middle of the lawn with a 12-inch, non-poisonous snake clamped down in the center of its body. The snake was moving on both sides. The next day, all I saw was a bit of the tail. How a small boy could eat that size snake amazed me. He soon graduated to bigger prey. Coming down my ramp, out of the corner of my eye, I saw what I thought was a dead bird. Getting closer, it was a headless squirrel. Vinny was nowhere to be found, but I sensed it was his doing. Tiger came over for a taste of the blood and walked away. By the time I got my sister to come outside and dispose of the squirrel, Vinny came out of the palms and retrieved his kill. As with the snake, in the same area, all that was left was the tail. He had no appetite for the plump mole. He was killing the beneficial critters, which I had no control over.

The fourth member of the wrecking crew was our neighbor's cat, who was left to fend for herself. At a younger age, she would walk the length of our side neighbor's fence to get to her home. I suppose they fed her but, when they moved, she was abandoned. We welcomed her as the fourth musketeer. As far as I know, she was not an assassin, merely a survivor.

Little Girl - 2019

Tiger liked to pick on her, I'm guessing, because she was smaller and vulnerable. She was taken by the harsh reality of the food chain — the coyote. Seeing them all gathered closely on the porch at feeding time, looking so innocent, waiting for their Grammy, was a morning and evening staple.

There were four bowls and water and, as mom finished her setup, they went for a random bowl, which was not how mom liked it. Rico was moved to position 1, Tiger 2, Vinny, bowl 3, and the abandoned white cat, who I named Little Girl, was picked up, along with her bowl, to a neutral corner so she could eat in peace, away from Tiger's bullying. After their meals, our survivors headed out into the elements, staking their claims under the hundreds of bushes and palms in the yard.

Tiger Woods - 2020

Vinny was the sweetest of them all. He communicated in his own language, chirping like a bird. I was convinced he was raised by a family of birds. In time, he picked up the local dialect. He would wait for my sister, who arrived home from work at 11pm. He sat patiently in the driveway or on top of the ramp to greet her. Rico was always purring and demanding affection. He had developed a unique talent for using the ramp door knocker that was shaped like a palmetto tree. After many months of practice, standing on his hind legs, tippy-toed, he grabbed that knocker and gave it a loud knock. He was relentless. Knocking until someone answered. He needed to see his mom, our mother. Vinny would jump on her stomach and knead her chest, sleep, purr, and do all the beautiful things that little innocent kitty cats do. King Rico succumbed to old age. He fought a 3-week battle, rarely eating or drinking. Tiger was diagnosed with cancer and there was nothing that could be done for him. The two arch enemies were euthanized weeks apart. I liked Tiger, but Rico was one of my favorites.

The last man standing was Vinny. The little boy who became a man reigned superior for two years, with no subjects. I wonder if he longed for the other cats in the crew? I know he loved my mother immensely. Vinny eventually received house privileges. We placed the litter box in the laundry room and he did his business there with no training or coaching. This smart, sweet boy loved to sit on the railings around the porch and my ramp. He knew he would be safe there and scope out any incoming enemy. He slowed his outside time the last month of his life. I was home alone at my computer station when I heard what sounded like a book falling from a shelf. I wish it was. Vinny had jumped up on a chair, then jumped onto the kitchen table. I'm guessing that he was trying to find a way down and the fall from the height of the table broke either a leg or a hip. There was no cry or scream, which surprised me. He wet himself a bit and started crawling towards the laundry room, twenty feet away. I tilted my chair to be closer to him and, through tears, in a calm voice, I asked him to please stop moving. "Vinny, it's OK, I'm calling your Grammy." He continued, making it to the litter box and used it to not soil the floor.

Through his pain, he was more concerned about not having a bowel movement on the wood floor. My mom and sister arrived home within ten minutes. Vinny was still in the litter box. Ellie picked him up, and I gave him a kiss on his forehead. They brought him to the vet. I had a strong feeling that he would not return — his injuries looked too severe. My mother loved him, and I know Vinny loved mom. Just a week before Vinny's passing, a small, multi-colored kitten appeared, and sat right next to Vinny on his cushioned chair. Vinny stared straight ahead after repeated attempts by this new kitten to grab his attention. He was sick and wanted nothing to do with her. I named her Missy. Another feral had made it to the big porch at number 947. We thought she would be a keeper and carry on the tradition of feral cats making their way to our home. It was not meant to be. After Vinny's passing, Missy was nowhere to be found. She was passing through or she had a home to go to. I thank her for her brief, caring moments with Vinny.

Chapter 32

Smoke Screen

The black smoke began wafting through the air conditioning ducts and engine cover as I reached the top of the James B. Edwards Bridge, crossing over the Wando River toward home. All of my van windows were closed, air conditioning on, when I began my sixteen-mile ride from class at Tech on I-526. Traveling with my best buddy Lee, my service dog, on a routine, hot-sticky summer day. My air conditioning picked the perfect location to crap out. The compressor was cooking as I had 1/4 of a mile to go to reach flat ground and find a secure place to pull my van over, deploy the lift, and find a way for Lee to exit safely without being hit by a speeding vehicle. As I drove faster, more smoke was drawn into the cabin. When we made it off the bridge, I realized the safety lane was too narrow to accommodate my van and the lift. If attempted, I would have to scream commands, hoping that Lee could hear over the passing cars. He understood my hand signs, but I could not take the chance of accuracy through the metal bracing on my lift. I had no other choice but to reach the first exit, which was close to one mile from the foot of the bridge. We were not coughing up our lungs from the smoke, but the cabin was getting dim. There was no option to open the windows. My hands could not come off of my tri-pin steering and acceleration pole when driving; that would launch a chain reaction of complete loss of control. My only option was to haul ass down to Long Point Road, find a place to stop and bail. A construction site occupied by a trailer was my first option, and I took it. Lord, please save me enough juice to get my side door open so at least Lee can exit. Yes, the van's systems were working! Lee got out on my command.

I gave Lee the sit-stay command, then I took the three-foot vertical ride down to ground level on the lift. I noticed a man exiting his vehicle and asked if he could spare a moment. "Yes, sir. How could I be of help?" I asked if he could open the driver's door and pop the lever so I could look inside the engine bay. She was still smoking a bit, and as he set the metal stick to keep the hood open, I immediately saw the cause of all the smoke. I knew the compressor had run out of refrigerant, but that was not the root cause of smoke filling the cabin. The engineer who designed my 1991 E150 van thought it best to put a one-inch thick, semi-hard, closed cell rubber pad for the compressor to rest on. I suppose it was an anti-vibration accommodation. You would think an engineer would consider, worst-case scenario on an engine design. A quarter round metal sleeve, possibly slow to heat titanium on top of the rubber, would have provided the consumer with a safety measure. Hell, incorporate asbestos in that rubber. Something! That van was like most Ford vans of that era; inadequate air conditioning. In our household, I am known as Mr. Safety. That's okay with me. I make sure our six doors that lead to the outside are double dead bolted locked. A two-minute exercise that gives me peace of mind. Water and food spills, mostly by me, are pointed out, annoyingly at times.

I asked my new friend if he thought it was safe to continue on. He said, "give it twenty minutes to let things cool and take the back roads home." Good advice - taken. He closed the hood down for me, and after I thanked him, he replied, "the Lord put us here to help one another." He teared me up and warmed my heart.

Chapter 33

Return to Paradise

I 'll spare you the boredom of the ship statistics — it's freaking huge! One year after my father's passing, I had the idea of a cruise to the Caribbean with a few of my family members. What started out as five quickly grew to sixteen. We cruised from Port Everglades in Fort Lauderdale to Nassau, St. Thomas, and St. Martin.

I had visited Nassau twice before, first as a 9-year-old, with our family, minus my older sister Michele, who had recently married. It was my first flight, done in style, aboard a Pan Am, Boeing 747 out of JFK. Back then, everyone dressed their best, and they served you an in-flight meal. We stayed at the quaint Beach Inn on the northern tranquil cove of Paradise Island. The sugary sand and crystal-clear water was new to us kids. The beach and adjacent area were our playground for the week. My younger sister Pat made it her practice to head down to the beach alone and get her own breakfast at the buffet. Quite independent for a 7-year-old!

I loved to explore and once ventured around the point from the beach and discovered a substantial pile of discarded mini speedboats. It was a peculiar sight, and I could only imagine how cool it would be if they were operational. Moving on, I found myself on the rugged, underdeveloped east-

Paradise Island - 1970

ern side of the island. The surf was rough, having no resemblance to our calm cove. Surely, something must have occupied this abandoned beach previously, because of the multiple sea urchin warning signs. Vacationers would soon populate this desolate beach upon completion of a new Holiday Inn, rising in the near distance. The Atlantis Resort was twenty-five years in the future.

Dad, Bill & me - Paradise Island - 1970

My second visit to Nassau was as a 23-year-old. I traveled solo and met up with my sister Ellie and her boyfriend Doug, aka, Mr. Franklin. It was my first and only visit to Cable Beach. I enjoyed cruising around New Providence in the back of the VW Bug that Ellie and Doug had rented. We had fun meeting their local friend Kelvin, BBQing on his blazing hot rooftop patio, and eating at local restaurants. I even danced — thankfully, there is no archive. Down toward the end of the beach, we rented a catamaran that we unintentionally flipped one mile offshore. We took turns with multiple dives to lower the sail that had its rigging slot oxidized. Our attempts were unsuccessful. Doug's foot was bleeding. Sharks were running through my head. We saw a small island that seemed close but, in the water, accuracy is fickle. Thoughts of swimming to it ceased when two sailors came by and assisted us with righting the cat.

Cable Beach - 1984

One evening, we crossed the bridge to party at Club Med on Paradise Island, which had changed somewhat, but not as drastically as my third visit via cruise ship in 2012. Getting to the port on time was crucial. Our road trip from South Carolina began a day early to allow for the unknowns. We stayed at a hotel near Port Everglades. On cruise departure day, our first order of business was to wait in line for our luggage and equipment handover. This is where my nerves became frazzled. To transfer from bed to wheelchair, we use an Easy Pivot lift, which operates on the lever-fulcrum principle. Without this piece of equipment, getting in and out, while doable, is difficult for everyone. The luggage and equipment handlers have been through this rodeo thousands of times before, but I had to approach the fella that had control of my lift. They secured it on a large apparatus, but I needed to speak with him. "Excuse me, can you please run me through the route that my lift will take to the ship?" He smiled, and replied, "I'm bringing it straight to a large holding room alongside the ship, where it will be handled and delivered by a second man, directly to your room. It's all tagged up. Don't worry, it will get there." I just needed to hear somebody who had authority say it.

The lift and my power chair were my two worries. I purchased insurance, just in case my health went south, and I needed to be airlifted back to the US. If my power wheelchair crapped out, I brought my manual chair as a backup. Yes, I'm a tad neurotic — in my business, if you're not, somewhere and sometime you will be screwed. I double check everything. I could finally relax when I entered my handicapped accessible room and saw my lift parked neatly in a corner. We should have brought bowling balls. There was more room than the three of us needed. Our large balcony on the fourteenth floor had a precision, wheelchair accessible ramp. The accommodations were stellar.

The Oasis of the Seas can accommodate 6,780 individuals. I thought that the common areas would be crowded, and we would have to elbow our way through. That was not the case. There was always more room than expected. The ship had fore-and-aft banks of elevators, each with eight cars. These were usually crowded during dinner service and activities after your meal.

This floating city had entertainment, multiple food choices, and services throughout. They had a full salon, so I splurged and had my hair cut. The major entertainment venue, the Opal Theater, at the front of the ship, accommodated 1,400 people. I loved my daily ritual of circling this behemoth's jogging track, which was 0.43 miles long, covered from the elements, and offered spectacular views. My wheelchair sped around that smooth, green ribbon at eight mph.

I had reserved a wheelchair accessible van that picked us up in the once-vibrant, downtown Nassau. My sister Ellie, who visited frequently with Doug, was shocked at its current condition. The ride through downtown had many boarded up, vacant businesses. I was told going in, that the downtown landscape had changed, but this was sad to see. It was a shell of itself, just another nondescript cruise port. Once over the bridge, it was a quick trip to the Atlantis resort, which had taken over most of Paradise Island. Atlantis had lured the masses — only a trace of what the island looked and felt like remained. If not for the blustery ocean wind snapping the blue, black, and gold of the Bahamian flag, we could have been in Vegas.

Aqua Theater on Royal Caribbean

Day tripping from the cruise ship had its time constraints. When we finished breakfast, negotiated the steep gangway, and traveled down the long pier, we had a six-hour window left to explore the new Paradise Island. Kelvin informed my sisters of a massive property being constructed on the site of his former employer at Cable Beach. Build big, survival of the largest, I suppose. They met up with him for lunch as our group of six ventured the opposite way. I had wonderful memories of my previous trips and was determined to seek out some in this new environment. Once inside the Atlantis mega-complex, we focused on the aquarium. They laid out the aquarium nicely and housed a variety of marine life. My favorite was the giant Ray. I was happy to see my mom snapping away with her new camera. We spent a few hours there, had lunch and met up with my private ride at three, to make it back to the ship by four.

Oasis of the Seas

We arrived at St. Martin on day six. There was a steady, light rain and, after four previous battles with the steep gangway, I enjoyed relaxing with mom on the ship's stern, which offered a beautiful view of the island. Earlier that morning, we discovered my bladder pressure meds had run dry. Murphy's law had reared its ugly head, withdrawal effects were now in play. I was angry with myself for this tenderfoot mistake, as I am the captain of my ship. My sister visited the ship's doctor, who gladly wrote a prescription for my 10mg slow-release medication. His departing words to her were, "Good luck, the Dutch are strict." Off Ellie went with my sister-in-law Irene, into the winding hills in search of my meds.

They were turned away by many pharmacies because our prescription was not written exactly as their stock of 3x intermittent pills, and the pharmacies wouldn't bend the rule. They took advice from a friend of Irene's. "Go to the clinic." After more than an hour there, a proper Dutch prescription for 3x intermittent pills was written and filled. They toyed with crossing to the French side of the island, but traffic could strand them. The ship waits for no one. The return cruise was a full day at sea, and we experienced more of the ship's offerings.

During my short stint at sea, I thoroughly enjoyed a play, the comedy club, and the spectacular diving performances at the Aqua Theater. It was my first cruise, and except for the gangway negotiation, I loved every bit! It has been several years since I've been to Nassau. Hopefully, the once vibrant downtown with all of its charm will return.

Chapter 34

The Amtrak Delight

The shock of our right rear tire exploding at 75 mph on a crowded I-95 a few days prior was still fresh in all of our minds. My sister Pat was at the wheel and switched into full NASCAR mode. She was losing power fast and had to get to safety, which was three lanes over. She maneuvered that wounded van around speeding vehicles, large and small. It was an amazing performance of her skills and bold decisions. She delivered our family to safety! After a moment of assessment, we called my road assistance company, who were beaten to the scene by a roving State Farm Insurance "Road Samaritan." We were quickly back on the road. My van sustained a shredded tire and damage to its rear air conditioning components. I needed a breather and had no desire to return home from Florida in the vehicle. I hired a transport carrier to bring it home.

I had taken my last flight years before and I promised myself to never return to that nightmare. Our only option to get back home was by Amtrak. I was excited. I've never been on a train, other than NYC subways and commuter rail into the city. I was looking forward to this new experience. I've heard from other train travelers that when you enter South Carolina, there were vast marshlands. The train ride was booked. I hired an accessible minivan for the two-mile drive to the train station. The van that was sent did not accommodate my tall body. I had to put my chair's backrest to a near flat position and power up the ramp backward into the minivan. The day was starting out peachy.

We arrived at the station and proceeded to the waiting area, which, thankfully, was air-conditioned. I was approached by a rail worker and was told that the train rarely pulls far enough forward on load ups, so I would have to board south of the platform and travel over tracks. I could not believe what I was being told. "Are we in the 19th century, am I being punked?" My consistent emergency carry is a bag of assorted pieces of wood. I call it "my bag o' wood." It has saved me many a time, crossing high thresholds. It was one of the items I took out of the van, as a possible need.

I traveled with my sister Michele to the end of the platform, onto hard packed dirt/gravel. We reached a concrete pad and placed the wood in between a track gap, emanating from a commercial building, rail siding and the main Amtrak line. You're probably thinking the same thing I did; this is pitiful, thirty years post the Americans with Disability Act. The wood worked. As is common in Florida, a thunderstorm can pop up at any moment. I looked to the east and saw one rolling straight towards us. We scrambled back to the shelter of the train station.

The fun ramped up. We were informed that we now had two hours to kill because someone thought up the brilliant idea of an insurance job, leaving their car on the northbound track in Miami. Yup, they stopped their car right on the track and walked away. The train hit the car and had to be extracted from underneath the engine. Wonderful, strike two! I always carry a tape measure with me and had my sister break it out to measure the aluminum wheelchair lift that was chained to an I-beam. It was folded up and I could only guess as to where my loading point would be. In my estimation, this contraption gave me about five inches of clearance. I was still puzzled as to how this device was going to work. I ran into the rail worker once more and asked if I could see the device unfolded. He was accommodating, unlocked the lift, and gave me a demo of how it was going to work. I now understood and breathed a little easier.

Finally, the train arrived, and we were fortunate that it pulled past the pad where I was going to board. I got on the lift and they cranked it up. I made it through the door with two inches to spare on either side. The day before, I saw a potential problem with my elbow rest that protruded from the armrest. We took the left one off, just as a precaution, and it paid off big time. Once on the train, they directed me to make a left and straight into our spacious private room. My sister Pat and I had a large, accessible compartment in the rear of the second to last car. The room had a large back area with two sleeper bunks, and up front was a large, three piece bathroom. A major piece of equipment was missing — there were no tie-downs for my wheelchair. That was hard to believe. Strike three, but the fun was far from over. Off we went. My sister Mary Ellen and my mom rode in coach, three cars ahead of us. They offered an option of a small two-person mini-suite. Regrettably, we did not go that route. Pat and I were all set, with Ellie and mom in their seats. Since the train was two hours late, the engineer drove that rambling wreck past its comfort zone, at least for me. With each subsequent stop, the train became crowded, and the restrooms got dirty. My expectations of beautiful scenery were brought down to earth. We saw enough impound yards, junkyards, and lumber yards to last us a lifetime. When these spectacular views were absent, we observed dense, characterless trees and brush.

So far, my power chair had not moved, which was miraculous. The train was hopping vertical, and lurching to the left and right. We thought, how in the world has this train not derailed yet? I watched the workers walking up and down the aisle being slammed against the walls. These people should have been given hazard pay. They were polite and very attentive to our requests. My only meal, a black bean hamburger, was delicious. The bobble-head doll that was quite popular when I was growing up in the 1960s — well, that's how I moved for ten hours. My body was in perpetual motion throughout the trip. Examining the schedule map that was given to us, we attempted to synchronize my catheterizations with our stops at the different stations. Well, you know that plan didn't work out well. When nature called, Pat was in gymnastic mode, inserting the catheter, making sure the collection tray did not fly off my chair and kept herself in an upright position at 75 mph. It would have made a great Saturday Night Live sketch. She was a trouper.

The journey was more taxing mentally than physically. I tried to get my mind into a comfortable state — a few breathing techniques helped. Pat and I talked a lot about memories of our fabulous dad. It was a grueling trip. Finally, we were within striking distance of our terminus at the North Charleston station. This stop was not in a good neighborhood, and I knew our train was the last one this night.

After our stop, it was only a matter of time before they closed the station. I belonged to an AAA sort of group that caters to disabled travelers. Their primary service was to have an accessible vehicle at my destination. I made the confirmation call two hours before our stop and was told that there was no ride. It fell through, and I was livid. Not good news at all. I thought of a way out of this situation that we were quickly approaching. My priority was the safety of my family. I made a call to the North Charleston Police Department and explained our predicament. They assured me that an officer would be waiting for us at the station. I was relieved and could relax a bit. Just knowing that we would be protected was a blessing.

The four of us made our way into the beautifully lit fluorescent station. We entered the parking lot and were greeted by the burly Officer Jim Ryan. The first thing he said was, "I wasn't sure who I would need, so I called in the cavalry." He certainly did! Officer Ryan introduced me to Charleston County's head EMT. She got right to business. "Mr. Waitzman, I have two options for you. We can transfer you into that SUV, or we can transfer you from your chair onto a gurney and into that ambulance." I opted for the ambulance. They had to retrieve a stored U-Haul type of trailer to transport my wheelchair home. They told me it could not be secured in the trailer. At that point, I didn't care if my chair arrived home in pieces.

Officer Ryan and the Charleston County EMT team took care of us. They delivered me and my family safely to our home in Mount Pleasant. When we arrived, I couldn't use my personal bed since I left my low-air loss mattress and motor in my van. The EMTs transferred me into my mom's spacious queen size bed. What a relief to be home. While we were waiting for the U-Haul, I got to talking with Officer

Ryan. I knew that he and the EMTs would not accept payment for this kind deed, so I asked them what their favorite local charity was. They told me and I gladly donated in their names. He told me he was in an organization that played the bagpipes. It intrigued me. I enjoy listening to the bagpipes but, to be frank, after three songs, I'm ready to move on. A group of my fabulous high school friends make an annual visit to Charleston. This has been a tradition for the past nine years.

There had been many losses in our collective families. I was planning a catered oyster roast for that October reunion, and I thought it would be wonderful if Officer Ryan could come and play Amazing Grace and a few other tunes. I called him and he immediately agreed. He told me he would only do it for free and he would refuse any sort of payment. We devised a plan that would surprise everyone. His shift began at 3pm that day, so 12pm would be a good time for him to show up. I told him that everyone would be in the backyard, and I'll call him from his staging position at the top of my street. We live on a corner and there is a small road leading to the houses behind ours. I told him to park there, and I would escort him through our fence where he would be in front of all the gang. I introduced him, gave a brief speech honoring our departed family members, and then Officer Jim played Amazing Grace.

We Miss You Shaheen

Chapter 35

Horlbeck

After I paid my two-dollar entry fee at the gate, I came upon the proverbial fork in the road and my choice was to the left. I departed the asphalt onto a hard-packed, sandy road, passing multiple rows of parking, nestled in thick woods. They thoughtfully designed the grounds, and I was still in the parking area of Palmetto Islands County Park. Traveling west, just beyond the elevated Park Center, is the tastefully constructed Splash Island, which superseded the dug-out swimming hole. At the end of the western portion of the trail, a long stretch of boardwalk crossed the salt marsh that connected to Nature Island.

It has no railings, so I always opted not to cross. Wide, accessible asphalt trails connect the nearly 950 acre park from one end to the other. Along this lush ribbon, there were jumping-off points of hard-packed mini trails into the salt marsh. These included lookouts. My favorite section of the park is the eastern side, which flows through more assortments of pines, palms, and thickets, eventually meeting up with Horlbeck Creek.

Palmetto Islands County Park - 2010

At this point, the trail curves north and runs parallel with the creek, which includes more outcropping trails with picnic tables. I enjoyed many fried chicken lunches with my family at these beautiful spots. At the end of this long trail was a dock, offering the opportunity to drop a ring net for blue crabs. Sister Pat is the crabber in the family, and she has had many successful outings. This wondrous setting was just down the road from Pat and Victor's first family home.

The park, with its abundance of natural beauty, has afforded us an outlet for enjoyment over the years. Here, I had come within thirty feet of my first sighting of a great blue heron, patiently stalking its prey, as well as an osprey nesting atop a service pole. This gem in our backyard shares a natural border with man's cruelty. Waterways in the South Carolina lowcountry were once used as highways for the indigo, rice, and cotton trade. Horlbeck Creek was one of many.

House Slave Cabins - Boone Hall Plantation

With the naked eye, our original sin is revealed in Boone Hall Plantation, where men, women and children were enslaved, living out their stolen lives in misery and despair. I have been to this plantation on a dozen occasions for events and visits with friends who came to town. When I have strolled the grounds, my thoughts were of the enslaved. I've wrestled with the appropriateness of events and visits on this hallowed ground — coming to the opinion that leans stronger toward the good that visits provided. Revenue from admissions keeps this and other plantations open to the public, where Gullah culture is kept alive through the storytellers. The brutality, suffering and resilience of the enslaved must continue to be taught, discussed, and never forgotten.

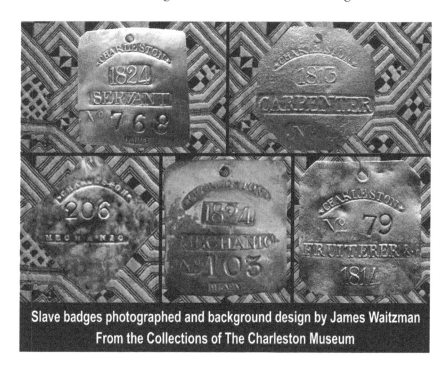

Slave badges photographed and background design by James Waitzman
From the Collections of The Charleston Museum

Chapter 36

The Creek

Brother Bill and I were on the boardwalk and, as he was snapping away, the Winds of Fortune entered Shem Creek. Music from the shrimp trawler filled the air as she headed directly towards us. Coming closer on a straight course, a concern rose between us.

Winds of Fortune

My thought was, no need to be alarmed. There's a professional captain at the helm. If loss of control was in play, a horn would have sounded. At thirty feet away, the captain turned starboard and slid his vessel to a spot on the other side of the creek. In the excitement, Bill could not get my phone into video mode quick enough to capture this beautifully choreographed docking maneuver. That late afternoon, he was able to capture a few stills of the storied shrimp boat.

Dad, mom, Lee and I moved to Mount Pleasant in the fall of 1993 and were later joined by my grandmother. My younger sister Pat and her family had already been in the lowcountry for several years. The first restaurant that we all went to was Shem Creek Bar & Grill on the backside of the creek. The restaurants had their acts together with ramps and elevators. Quite impressive, three years after the ADA had become law. I have dined at nearly all of these establishments, which are good, but mom, my sisters- and brother-in-law cook so well, we just need the catch from the fleet.

Back then, if you wanted to enjoy a view of the creek, you had to go to a restaurant or transverse the three-foot-wide sidewalk on the Coleman Boulevard bridge. Foolishly, I did it once and there is no room for error. The town finally constructed an accessible dock renovation that included a boardwalk along the creek and over the salt marsh that extends to Charleston Harbor. The town made subsequent additions, with rampage from the dock to the bridge on Coleman Boulevard extending to the opposite side of the creek. Now, there was access to the restaurants without putting yourself in danger. It was a much-needed addition that opened up the creek for all to enjoy.

Fresh, local shrimp is one of two reasons for a trip to the creek. For many years, our go-to purveyors for the tasty crustacean were C.A. Magwood Jr. & Sons and the Wando Shrimp Company.

Fresh, wild caught shrimp.

You had the option of heads on or off and Wando froze enough to sell throughout the off season. Tarvin Seafood currently sells at the Wando dock, which is supplied by their trawlers' Miss Paula and Carolina Breeze. Mt. Pleasant Seafood is another fine choice. Our family enjoys a couple pounds per week, more when we have guests. Why a local would buy anything but local is beyond my comprehension.

Eating farmed shrimp that was raised in an antibiotic-laden pond is not my idea of a healthy choice. Aquaculture is on the move in our backyard too, with farming standards that are superior to Southeast Asia and Central American producers. As long as there is a local supply, I'll stick with wild caught. Is wild sustainable in the long run? Let's hope so.

Will I ever embrace aqua farmed, US shrimp? Rigid standards and regulations with inspections would have to be met. That is a big ask when our current poultry, pork and beef regulations don't cut the mustard. Sadly, the creek fleet has dwindled from its heyday of seventy-five trawlers to its current handful. High fuel prices, hard winter freezes that delay season openings, high insurance rates and consumers opting for the aforementioned poor choice have been painful for the industry. Hopefully, a quick ride over to the creek to purchase a few pounds will never cease.

A little piece of paradise

My creek — is the pelican and gull, vying for bycatch from a returning shrimp boat at day's end.

My creek — is the dolphin that passes through in search of sustenance.

My creek — is the minnow, feeding in the pluff mud depressions in the salt marsh at low tide.

My creek — is the solitude at the end of the park, sighting an elegant egret, flying home to its roost at dusk.

Despite all the hustle and bustle of restaurant row and our overuse, nature abounds. All one must do is slow down and observe.

The shrimp trawler, "Winds of Fortune", was sold in July 2020.
RIP Captain Wayne Magwood.

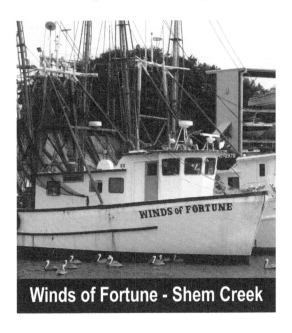

Chapter 37

Bivalve

I enjoy oysters steamed, fried, baked, or raw. My preference is steamed. We call steamed, here in South Carolina's lowcountry, "roasted." The oysters that are harvested and enjoyed in these waters are the Eastern Oyster. At a roast, they are mostly served in a cluster formation. These clusters typically have five to twenty or more oysters fused together in varying sizes and are steamed open and served hot. The hassle of prying the shell open is done for you, courtesy of the steam box or pot. You need not get all fancy with equipment — you can break down larger clusters, place them on a grill or grate, then cover with wet burlap. Basic, but effective. That's the method my neighbor used at my first roast twenty-nine years ago. Lowcountry oyster roasts take place from September to the end of April.

My favorite place for an oyster roast is at Bowens Island. I love the rustic charm, spectacular marsh, and sunset views. It gets crowded, so we always arrive early. I prefer my roasted oysters on Sunday at Bowens. The main restaurant is closed, but there are many Sundays when a local organization has a fundraiser.

Sunday Oyster Roast at Bowens

These events usually take place down over the water in the oyster shack, which can accommodate about two hundred. The overflow bivalve lovers enjoy theirs outside. We once had the pleasure of mass consumption under the main restaurant on a Sunday. Although I enjoy being down on the water, I prefer the space and warmth underneath the restaurant.

My sister Mary Ellen and I have been meeting up with our friends, Nathacia and Gerald, on Sunday roasts for many years. Ellie does a darn good job of shucking on a cluster. Nathacia breaks out her stubby, pointed knife and will dig down into the center. If she sees a newbie struggling, school is in session.

Nathacia and Gerald

Most Sunday roasts run from 1 to 5pm, with a full house at 2. A bit after 3, the crowd thins, and the heavy hitters are all that remain. That's when we are in our stride. I'm tapped out when my tongue has reached its salt saturation level. Usually, that would be at seventy-five oysters, give or take. My favorite roast is the Sierra Club fundraiser. They serve ice cream, which gives much needed relief to my salty tongue. Another bonus of Sunday roasts is the live music, which is bluegrass, country, and reggae fusions, performed by local musicians.

My love of oysters with great friends would not be complete without letting you know about my wonderful family, whom I have been blessed to know since high school. In 2010, this fabulous group of friends started an annual visit to our little piece of paradise. From California, Arizona, New York, Massachusetts and Connecticut, friends came and come.

Coined by my best bud, Bill, "Operation Visit Jim Waitzman" has been a consistent joy in my life. Our reunions usually run from Thursday to Tuesday in mid-October. We have enjoyed quite a few of the variety of restaurants in and around Charleston these past nine years.

Gastronomically speaking, the one common denominator is the oyster. We have enjoyed roasts at Bowens and in my backyard, steamed to perfection by Big Gerald. Pearlz, on the peninsula, is a main go-to spot, as well as Leon's on upper King, where we enjoy them raw or fried. I don't imbibe, but those oyster shooters that the crew knocks down at Pearlz sure look inviting. Covid has thrown a wrench into our annual reunion these past three years. We enjoyed having Laurel visit last fall. Hoping that we can return to our annuals with the entire crew in the near future. There are a whole lotta oysters that need to be shucked.

The Crew

Chapter 38

Cuisine

T hroughout my life, I have encountered a fair number of foreign objects in my food. This story details my most prominent memories.

When we first moved to Mount Pleasant, across the Cooper River
from Charleston, we did quite a lot of restaurant exploration. On
one hot, humid summer day - common weather here - my mom,
Lee and I ventured across the erector-set bridges to the peninsula.
Parking, if you are not in the loop or have never visited, is horrible. I
found inadequate handicapped surface parking, south of what was
then the Omni Hotel. We had a four-block stroll to our destination.
We were set to have lunch at a new establishment named FISH.

Our first mistake was even being out in the midday sun and humidity. Our chosen route was straight up King Street. The restaurant
received great reviews and was one of the first in the transformation
of upper King Street. Affordable college dorm furnishings, as well
as a few high end furniture stores, dominated the street for many
years.

We finally arrived at our destination, one block north of Marion Square. It was a welcome relief to sit in the air conditioning. We had a bowl of water put down for Lee, but as usual, he never cared to drink while out and about. I'm guessing his preference for the taste of home water was strong. It was lunch, but the volume was light as we perused the menu. Mom and I decided on the gumbo.

As was customary, my mother covered me with napkins. I can be a messy eater sometimes. Next, my wrist brace, which accepts a fork from a 180° swiveling cuff, was strapped on. Okay, time to begin with our meal — aw, shit! I have had a dry spell, but it's now over. Waitress, can you come over, please? Yes, how can I be of help? Well, look at my bowl and you be the judge. "I see it, not quite doing the backstroke, is it?" I'm guessing that the fly had a glorious death, drowning in the spicy gumbo. Fortunately, for me, I spotted the little beast before I put spoon to mouth.

I searched the menu for a replacement of the adulterated dish. "Please tell me what you have in a whole food form. Nothing chopped up, preferably a whole fish, grilled." She came back from the kitchen with offerings of tuna or swordfish. I ordered the tuna, rare. We left and the comfortable room that had provided us with respite from the brutal Charleston weather. We were back in the elements on our reluctant return trip to my van.

On the way back, we took another route, one block east on Meeting Street. We were more than halfway, and made a stop at the old firehouse to catch some shade next to the engines, where Lee was offered a bowl of water and customarily declined the drink. We had one long block to travel to the Omni Hotel, where we planned to cool off for an hour. Mom and I were attempting to relax and meditate in the comfort of the cool lobby when a passerby interrupted us and wanted to know everything about me and Lee. My first inclination was to tell him that this was not a good day for conversation, but being the over polite, accommodating person, I engaged in conversation for nearly an hour with this gentleman. Our batteries were charged and homeward we went. Lesson relearned of how dangerous the combination of heat and humidity was to our bodies. My spinal cord injury has left me without the ability to perspire from my chest to my toes. I knew better, rookie mistake.

Jumping back to my able-bodied days in NY, my girlfriend always liked to hit Jones Beach, West End 1 or 2. They are the longest walk from the parking lot to the ocean but, wanting to please, I tolerated the hot sand walk. This was many years before my injury, and since I was in shape, it was no big deal. It became time to walk back to pick up a couple of hot dogs at the food pavilion. I returned without taking a bite of mine and we began to eat. My tombstones stopped abruptly as I bit into something hard, less than one quarter of an inch from the outside of the dog. Oh, yes, we have something foreign in my dog. I've come across the occasional bone chip in a dog, but this was epic. My dissection uncovered a piece of bone the length of the last joint of my index finger. Yup, about an inch long, carpenter pencil wide. I was more fascinated than nauseated. How can a piece of bone that large pass through to the ending process of the manufacture of this hot dog? I buried the bone dog.

Many years ago, I adopted a new personal rule: never dine in poorly lit restaurants. Being a pescetarian for over fifteen years, I knew that certain species of fish have small to large amounts of bone that you must navigate through. It's to be expected in its natural form. I have developed extensive tongue training to sort out the bones, knowing their locations that I might miss on the plate.

The sacred mint Girl Scout cookie broke my heart one evening. As I looked down at the freshly opened wrapping, I noticed a half-inch tuft of rodent hair, anchored to the chocolate dipped lusciousness. That moment ruined a lifetime relationship. I'm a realist and there are guidelines in food production set by the government, but that big bone in the dog still blows my mind. I've been fortunate to never have cracked a tooth. My bag of dried prunes states they are pitted, one should never assume, and chomp hard on those goodies without caution. Again, that is its natural form and there is a possibility — I'm cool with that.

If you have read what our government permits within their stated pure food guidelines, you'll never eat again. Yes, wheat, grain, and cereals will have bits of friendly insect pieces incorporated within, but you must eat. Just think of it as granola. I'll never know what I was reincarnated from, but it must be interesting having these encounters with food. I've always enjoyed vegetables and made a point to get a couple of scoops of peas on my tray, on the job, in the various corporate buildings that I worked in. As I was munching on my lunch, I spooned up some peas and bit down on a small, pebble like material. I missed this one. Surprisingly, my molar was intact. I called over the food and beverage manager, who made it a point to hang around at the construction worker's table. He was shown the foreign object, and he gave me a weasel giggle, not addressing the seriousness of my complaint. I was twenty-two, had a secure, well-paying job, which stopped me from grabbing this ass by the neck and have him experience the pebble. I would have lost my job, even though he was a contractor, too. He had the suit and tie, and I was a Lee Rider, t-shirted carpenter in a corporate environment. The pebble bothered me, but what enraged me was his casual attitude, lack of respect, and not even offering a free lunch or two.

A mile south of our home is a long-established barbecue joint. I traveled with dad and Lee in the drive-through, placed our order, negotiated the narrow turn, where dad paid and picked up our order from the rear window. We liked to drive a few blocks south and eat in the van under a large live oak. Lee, my service dog, would take my nylon lunch bag to the back of the van where my father sat in the captain's chair. Dad would transfer my pulled pork sandwich into the bag and command Lee to take it. I would then give Lee the command to come to me at the driving station. He held the bag until I could get a hold of the strap, give him a good boy, and he was off to the back to get his reward from my father.

On all occasions when we ate at Wendy's hamburgers, Lee would get the four corners of my dad's double bacon cheeseburger. The barbecue that we had that day did not go well with Lee's tummy. He had to settle for bits of ice and a milk bone. Reaching over to the passenger seat, I grabbed and squared up my lap board to accommodate my mustard-based, South Carolina style, pulled pork sandwich. Removing the top of the bun to tuck in the meat neatly, to my surprise, there was a good old, quarter sized, half-inch-thick piece of bone, smack dab in the middle of the sandwich. I'm no longer shocked to see these bonus goodies in my food. I'm just happy that I opened the sandwich, and the hunk of bone was on top and not mixed in with the heap of shredded pork. Yeah, that one turned my stomach. I waited until dinner to eat. How the hell does someone miss a piece of bone that freaking large? I'll never know. Was it deliberate? I sure hope not. I have more trust in humankind to think that somebody would do that on purpose. Most likely, a non-thinker, as dad would often say.

Hair, glorious hair. This is probably the most prevalent of non-food items that people come across in their food. I was munching on some local, freshly made Mediterranean food, stuffed in a pita. We cut it in half; I ate half and made my way to the remaining piece. After a few bites, my cheeks had an equal amount of food as my tongue identified something odd. Oh no, is this fishing line? No, unless it's a very thin monofilament. I mumbled to my sister to come over and look into my mouth. Do you see that hair like thingy? She did and slowly pulled out a ten-inch-long hair extension. Jackpot, my first hair extension! Not surprisingly, she lost her appetite. I brushed off the main dish but scarfed down the beans and a salad. Usually, I get repulsed and break camp from the table — that day was an anomaly. We never have incidents with home cooking. I certainly don't miss the gristle and bone in the hamburger and hot dog. I try to eat food that is not processed, but the hair is only avoidable if the prep worker or cook slicks back their hair or wears a hat or net on their head. There is nastiness out there, but we must eat.

Bon appétit.

Chapter 39

Extra Fun

Yes, I would love to walk and run again. I run like a gazelle in my dreams, but given the lengthy list of all the extras that come and develop with SCI, I'd pick a few others first if I had choices. Spasms have been the bane of my existence as a paralyzed man for close to 38 years. My dragon craves attention — demands more, with little resources that I can fight back with. My dragon has been a constant companion from day one of my injury. Arriving subtly manageable, in most occurrences. As I have aged, my beast has become relentless at times, leaving me debilitated and hopeless.

I have dealt with spasms in various forms; clonus, trunk arches, extensor, flexor, and full body-all out hell. Early on, I have had the occasional spasm at various areas of my body, below my C5 injury location without a care. I drove for many years, always conscious when potholes or rough roadway that could trigger a spasm and send me out of control of my vehicle. Stretching exercises helped to prepare for the ride and I paused to keep my body limber. I did not experience any major problems until I purchased a new van that was fully, electronically controlled through a "drive by wire" setup. They built my previous adaptive vehicles with manual, mechanical levers and fulcrums, with the exceptions for electronics that locked down my wheelchair and controlled lights, air conditioning, shifting, and such. The "drive by wire" van was more of a challenge. Its sensitivity had to be toned down for my liking. I preferred the feel of the mechanical system; although my arms and shoulders ached daily driving home from Florida to New York, after a night's return from Myrtle Beach and the long drive to Asheville from Yonkers.

After a few months of driving the new style van, my health took a turn for the worse. I had increased spasms and also developed heart issues. My sisters and brother could drive the van — I backed away from the wheel for the safety of myself and others. These new, more frequent and powerful spasms changed my life in ways that I could never have imagined. I had bouts of my lower limbs kicking and thrashing about in the middle of the night, waking me up and eventually leave me out of a comfortable sleeping position. That involved waking up a family member in the dead of night. I did what most quads do when situations such as this arise. Drop off a urine sample to see if any infections were present. I had made it a habit to have a kidney and bladder ultrasound each year to check if any stones in my kidneys had formed, moved, or gotten stuck in my plumbing. I am an incomplete quadriplegic; meaning that I have touch sensation below my level of injury which is midway down my neck (C5). I scheduled an ultrasound and a CT scan, and examination of my toenails for any ingrown ones, which had put me in the hospital for three days, one year post injury. Any irritation below my injury, which includes a simple, ingrown toenail, can set my body into autonomic dysreflexia, commonly referred to as AD.

I had my first bout with AD 1 1/2 years after injury. It was an ordinary afternoon, getting cleaned up by my CNA Benny, and out of nowhere, my head felt tremendous pressure, as if vises were being tightened on all sides. I thought that my body could not possibly tolerate a second more. At that moment, with that pain, I was ready to check out. I have never felt pain that intense. They rushed me to a local hospital where they were able to bring my blood pressure to a manageable number. My God, the relief was a blessing that I still cherish today. The rehab staff taught us about AD and informed us it usually comes on early in your injury. Since that day, I have never suffered from an episode as intense as that afternoon. All courtesy of an ingrown toenail. From that day, I have regularly visited my podiatrist every eleven weeks. For many years, I asked the Lord for another day without AD. Many years later, I had a dime sized kidney stone we monitored for years. It must have become bored hanging out in the center of my right kidney. It rambled from its resting place into my ureter and set up camp for three days. My AD kicked into gear, thankfully at a moderate pain scale. Surprise, it was a Friday, when most wonderful medical occurrences happen. My urologist asked if I could make it to Tuesday. If the pain got any worse, get to the ER. That was a big ask. Naively, I complied. He lasered the stone. That is when I became smarter when yielding my health to a doctor.

My spasm battle three years ago was the worst my dragon brought; complete spasm takeover of my body, below my neck. Every muscle in my body, ones that I have not moved in years, were now on a mission. My dragon hijacked my body and sanity. I was desperate, my family was desperate. We had to wait two weeks to get an appointment at the SCI clinic downtown. ERs were full of Covid patients. This was the beginning of COVID-19 and its march across the world. I found the best masks online that my sister and I could afford, or get our hands on. I had a forty-five minute wait to see the physician. Solace was a cubicle away. During my two week wait, I spent my days and nights in a fetal position. My thighs mimicked a gymnast — positioned, held, as close to my torso as possible. My sisters arranged pillows in very imaginative ways. That was the only position that gave me moments to breathe easier, have cold rags placed on my beet-red face, and catch a respite back into sanity. Throughout those two weeks of hell, I drank ice water and ate yogurt. I knew the ride down to Charleston was going to be miserable. My hands were in a lock tight position. I could only move my wheelchair by poking at the joystick, which propelled me in one foot increments. It scared me to grab onto it, fearing that my hand could not break free, and I would crash into the brick exterior of our house at the bottom of the ramp. It took me an hour to cross the road from the hospital parking lot, into the building, and up to the 6th floor.

The doctor saw my condition. He knew how distressed I was and filled a prescription of Valium, which unfortunately is one of the few drugs for spasm relief available in the state that I reside. Here in the progressive state of South Carolina, organic relief, if you get my gist, does not exist. The pharmaceuticals worked. By the second day, I finally got that long wished for, full night's rest, sans spasms. I'm sure my mom and sisters enjoyed having my dragon gone. My three beautiful sisters and mother watched over me, and when the constant spasms came to their end, it was a rebirth, an overwhelming joy that the physical and mental trauma had left. I'm a realist and I knew there would be another occurrence in the future. As I write this piece, I am in the closure of another spasm clash that was far less traumatic to the full, no holds barred battle from three years ago. It was powerful enough to prevent me from performing my job. An additional drug, Zanaflex decreased my dragon's strength.

It worked, but the dosage was too strong, generating daily fainting, without warning. Seven in one afternoon. Once, I fainted for fifteen minutes in my van. They lowered the dose, and I have strung along six days without the vapors. We thought we were on a road to stability with my medication. The sudden fainting returned. Back to the local ER, another CT, which showed nothing abnormal. They then took me downtown to MUSC, where Ellie and I spent 48 hours of brain scans for seizures and stroke. A full pacemaker evaluation, and a three-dimensional heart scan. All tests were negative. I had a one on one with a resident to discuss a heart drug named Florinef that I have been taking each morning for twenty-seven years. My blood pressure is low, a result of my paralysis. I am usually 100/60. As we brainstormed further, she concurred with my thought that with the added Zanaflex, the Florinef dosage needed to be studied. In an hour, the cardiac team returned and suggested a test to monitor my blood pressure with the Florinef split into .05, twice a day in place of the 1.0 once a day. We received significant results. Now, I take a morning dose and a late afternoon dose when most fainting occurred. So far, so good.

It no longer disturbs me, knowing that another spasm episode is in my future, always on my dragon's terms. I now have more tools in my box, albeit limited to continue to be my best.

I thought forty sessions of radiation, six years ago, would eradicate my prostate cancer, until a yearly check, two years post, showed elevated numbers. A PET scan revealed it spread. I was pissed, but I brought myself into perspective and thought about the children at St. Jude, my primary charity. I have lived a very full life, before and after SCI. I began long term injectable prostate cancer treatment and will continue as long as it works. It keeps me alive. I'm grateful.

I'll close with a funny story, at least I found it entertaining. In February 2022, still under Covid's restrictions, I had a bit of a cough, nothing that I thought was unusual. I pacified my family, who deserve to know my condition, especially during a pandemic period. Charleston County EMS brought me over to the ER to get an X-ray. No family was permitted, just me and the X-ray tech. Sister Ellie joined me after the X-ray. The cassette was being examined by the tech, and I heard this non-thinker blurt out, "oh, damn, I've never seen that before." I was obviously alarmed, the doctor came in and told me what was going down. I saw the screen where my left lung was supposed to be, looking like a white piece of paper. Knowing from experience that all white on an X-ray is not an excellent color. The doctor told me I had a collapsed lung. I felt perfectly fine. Now I have thoughts running through my head that I'm gonna lose my left lung. Twelve years prior, I nearly lost my right lung. They drew one liter of fluid out, not knowing how or why. My lung did not drop after the fluid removal. I had a pleural effusion, requiring the pleural lining to be removed. Coming out of the anesthesia from that six-hour surgery to remove the lining was rough. I heard multiple voices, the surgeon being the most familiar. I have undergone many surgeries. This one kept me in the foggy middle zone for a long time.

It was a different kinda limbo. I surely welcomed the relief of clarity. The bonus prize was having the plastic airway shank removed from my nostril. Through the skilled hands of the surgeon, the operation was a success.

I asked the doctor if I was gonna lose my left lung. I was prepared for the bad news. Collapsed sounds so final. "No, no, you are going to work with the pulmonology team and rehab your lung back into shape." I never knew that a collapsed lung could be rehabilitated.He got me upstairs in ten minutes and I was being worked on by the respiratory team right away. They got busy on me, performing quad coughs, which is a synchronized exercise between myself and the therapist. They thrust a heavy towel onto my diaphragm as I attempt to cough in synchronization. It works, and it works well if it's done with precision. I told the team that I believed eye contact would be the best way to start, they agreed. I wore them out; I would do fifty reps each visit, which was usually every three hours. On my second visit by the head of the team, he asked if I had any aversions to having a plastic tube inserted into my windpipe and lung. No, not at all. I'm here to work, so whatever you ask, I will do. This tube was narrower than my previous experience, from a neck surgery in1987. I can't explain what it feels like swallowing plastic and the tube probing your lung. Let's just say that your gag reflex is extremely heightened. There is a reward when you hear the tube suck out the stubborn phlegm. Before we started, I told the therapist that I'm gonna give it fifteen seconds and if I can't handle it, I'll touch your left hip for the tap out. That wasn't necessary. He got in, did what he had to do and we teamed up for another probe the next afternoon. He told me that twice was the stopping point, and he would not need to go in for anymore. The quad coughs continued for three days, performed by talented respiratory therapists that should be proud of the profession that they chose.

Most times when I visit a hospital unexpectedly, I bring all my medication so the pharmacist can compare with what they have on their shelf. This is a long process, and sometimes, you're not gonna get your meds at the same time that you get your meds when they are under your control at home. I've been taking a spasm drug Baclofen as far back as I can remember. It doesn't do much, but it's still in my rotation. I've weaned down over the years and was in the process of another wean down when I landed for this mini vacation. My Baclofen got lost in the mix, which is a big no - no. When admitted to the hospital, your meds take time to get on the floor and administered. I blame myself. It's my responsibility. What occurred was my first trip into the realm of withdrawal. 2 1/2 days without my Baclofen sent me into a world of non reality. I was told that I was speaking erratically and not answering questions directly posed to me. All I remember was that the room looked different, not drastically, but different enough for me to become uncomfortable. My sister Ellie came to my side, and I asked her for a drink. She brought me water, and I spat a mouthful onto the left side of her jacket. She immediately asked me why the hell I did that. When she approached me at first, the whites of her eyes were dark red, which frightened me. I didn't ask why she had blood-red eyes, I just spat. I figured that if she was truly not my sister that she would melt, as all witches do when water hits their body. I also believed that I would have protection from any non-human force, being that electronics and water don't go well together. The doctor entered the room and restored order. I lingered in a peculiar state. They figured out the medication screw-up, and I finally received a lower dose of Baclofen. That's my mini hallucination wrapped up in a paragraph.

Chapter 40

Service

I heard through a local media outlet that Westchester County Airport was once again hosting two bombers that were based in Britain during World War II. These types of aircraft were in the Pacific, as well. My father served as a radio operator strike caller in the Pacific Theater from 1943 to 45, with the 292nd Joint Assault Signal Company (JASCO).

B-24 Liberator

We traveled the short distance to the airport and spent the afternoon. The volunteer crew and many team members had these beauties fine-tuned for flight. We were fortunate to see the B-17 land and taxi our way.

Dad left his comfortable college life at Cornell University after his freshman year and enlisted — he told his parents that he was drafted. He reported to the Atlantic

City Convention Center, where they processed him and issued his gear. His next stop was central Florida for basic training and then onward to Pittsburgh for radio operator school. He spoke with such admiration for the people of the Iron City. From there, he boarded a train to Washington State and sailed to Hawaii for jungle training. The war awaited him in Asia.

Dad never spoke of his service un-less I asked him, which I often did, but I never delved into a specific subject I thought would box him in. As a kid, I was surely tempted to blurt out, "Dad, did you ever kill a guy?" Every little kid would want to know that. I always felt it

292 JASCO - Jungle Training - Hawaii 1943

was not my place to ask. Dad was awarded the Bronze Star, which always piqued my curiosity. It was in a rectangular box, along with his dress uniform in the attic. As an adult, I tried on a few occasions to learn of the details regarding the medal. The last time that I asked was when I was working at an awards shop here in Mt. Pleasant. I had his Bronze Star mounted in a shadow box for a proper display. He appreciated it, but dad would not go there. He took that memory and others with him. SSG Sidney Miller Waitzman was on a ship in Tokyo Bay as The Instrument of Formal Surrender of Japan to the Allied Powers was signed aboard the USS Missouri.

He finished out his service to our country in occupied Japan and then sailed home. Dad told me of a lone man on a bluff, who greeted them with a wave as his troop ship entered the Columbia River. That simple gesture touched him. I could hear it in his voice. As my Uncle

Duane told me, "Your dad boarded the train in Washington, crossed the country, then took the commuter train from Grand Central, getting off at Tuckahoe and walked the mile up the hill to home, modestly, without fanfare." When Uncle Duane spoke those words, it did not surprise me at all. That is how my dad lived his life.

Dedicated to the men of the 292nd Joint Assault Signal Company
77th Infantry & 1st Cavalry Divisions
who regulated ship to shore air strikes

GUAM — LEYTE — LUZON
IE SHIMA — OKINAWA — JAPAN

Occupied Japan - Kawasaki 1945

Chapter 41

My Family

My family rushed like bees back to the hive when they received the news. Some members of my family were waiting in the emergency room before the helicopter landed on the 34th Street helipad. I was anxious to know about my official diagnosis. I knew I had a cervical injury, but the extent of it was not yet defined. By midnight, they diagnosed me as a C5 incomplete quadriplegic. I still retained most touch sensation below my upper chest. Hearing the advantage of being an incomplete quad was meaningless to me. A cornerstone to build from, perhaps — my mind was still in survival mode.

I spent one week in the ICU, then transferred to the floor at Bellevue Hospital on 1st Avenue at East 26th Street in New York City. I was now exposed to an area that unfortunately included the hallway wanderers, of which there were many. They included a combination of patients, visitors, and trespassers. Twice, I had wanderers approach me in my room, with my Halo gear on, attempting to bum a smoke that I did not possess. On both occasions, my roommate, who was able-bodied, jumped up from his bed and barked, "get your ass out of this room."

My "bodyguard" took care of my safety that first week. No charge. I told him to choose whatever was on my food tray. I was at the yogurt and liquid stage. My folks hired a private duty nurse for the rest of my stay. I was in Bellevue for three weeks and transferred to NYU's Rusk Rehabilitation, just up First Avenue at 34th Street. From day one, and throughout my four-month stay, at least one family member and a few close friends were a constant presence. It was uplifting to see them and they brought me delicious food. They dedicated a chunk of their salaries to the "feed Jim food fund." Traveling down to the city to care and comfort me was a tremendous emotional strain on my family and friends. They never showed it. I was in their safe, loving cocoon.

After a few weeks at rehab, I shot a high fever and felt extremely ill. The remedy that the nurses implemented was to ice up my entire body. Success, my fever went down, but now I was shivering uncontrollably for nearly two days. My jaw muscles took the brunt. They seized up tight. I was told in the evening a specialist would come and evaluate my situation. His prep, "I am going to firmly place my thumb between your lower lip and chin, then I will forcefully push downward and it's going to be painful." He gave me a moment to prepare for the festivities and told me to tell him when I was ready. In a few seconds, through my clenched mouth, I said go. That was the second most painful moment I had endured. It came close to having the four screws driven into my head when the Halo was installed, but it did not meet that full threshold of pain. Thankfully, his thumb was grinding into my chin for only a moment. "You'll be fine. Give it a few days — muscle fatigue." He clicked his heels and exited.

Life went on and, in a couple of days, I was back on my rehab schedule. I still hadn't regained use of my atrophied shoulder and bicep muscles. The occupational therapist told me, once I get them back, they would fit me with an orthotic and I'd be able to feed myself. I had my doubts, but I was in the right place and I would not quit. It was only a matter of time and perseverance, and I was feeding myself independently. That felt good, damn good — I gained some semblance of independence in rehab.

There was one piece of equipment that everybody feared. The dreaded tilt table. Spending a lot of time in bed hindered my body from being accustomed to a seated position. They strapped me to a padded table at the ankles, knees, thighs, hips, and chest. The next step - I was being tilted upright by the rehab therapist - slowly. I began flat on the table at 0°, first stop 20°, which was tolerable, then 40°, still cool. Now, the fun started at 60°. For my initial session and subsequent five, I came to the cusp of pass-out territory - not an enjoyable place to be. The next words that came out of my mouth were, I'M DONE! In time, my body acclimated.

My family was interested in what I did every day and we talked about coming home for part of the day, which we accomplished with only a few hiccups. It was both joyful and sorrowful. As I entered through the front door, the staircase leading up to the second, then the third floor, was in plain sight. Ten steps away that I would never take. Most of my possessions were in my third-floor bedroom. I had already been stripped physically, now this stark reality. One more hit that I had to absorb, deal with, and move past. We had a nice family dinner and by 8pm I was back at Rusk rehab.

December 18th - time to begin my new life as a paralyzed man in the world. They taught me well in rehab. My mom was a nurse, my sister Mary Ellen was in the radiology field, along with her husband Doug. My sisters Michele and Pat picked up on my healthcare needs in rapid time. After settling in the first-floor sunroom, my main craving was to go for a long cruise of my old stomping grounds. My sisters drove me anyplace I asked - I was desperate for some sense of normalcy. Walter's hot dogs, Greasy Nick's burgers, and City Island seafood stoked my new normal.

From the spring of 1987 through the spring of 1988, my mom took a leave of absence from her nursing job. My dad had since retired from the auto parts export business. The three of us flew to Florida after they accepted me into a rehab study at the Miami Project to Cure Paralysis. We were fortunate that my mom's cousin Wesley had an apartment in Hollywood. Ellie drove her car down for us to use on our three day per week therapy schedule. At first, I took part in an upper body functional electrical stimulation (FES) study that lasted four months. Being in downtown Miami afforded us the opportunity to cruise the area. I loved the art deco hotels that lined Ocean Drive and lounging in the warm waters off of Key Biscayne where the views of Miami were spectacular. My attendance was perfect in the upper body sessions, and I was approached to see if we could stay in the area and pedal the ERGYS electrical stimulation bicycle. My mom had her leave extended for me to take part in the program.

My entire family has been involved in my paralyzed life. Ellie's husband Doug, God bless his departed soul, was always there for me. He passed down words of wisdom when he saw I was becoming too aggressive toward my mom and dad. From the beginning, my parents and siblings were my caregivers, with a few breaks when mom and dad needed a NY trip. Ellie, Shelley, and Pat always made sure I was clean, dressed, catheterized, and my bowel routine was done.

Ellie, our Chief of Staff, lives in the "west wing," - runs operations, and has become my barber since Covid. She does a far better job than the old place up the street. All cook for me and mom. Oldest sister Michele is our Costco Queen, keeping us stocked for months. My brother-in-law Victor prepares delicious meals, helps me whenever I ask, and I enjoy his funny, quick wit and conversation. Pat is always a phone call away to visit, help, or get me out of a jam. Brother Bill and husband John make their visit each October. Brother Doug and his wife Irene have generously supported the Miami Project to Cure Paralysis, as well as Canine Partners for Life, for many years. All my sisters are proficient in my health care needs, which is not always a picnic. Nanny, my departed grandmother, was kind, helpful and very independent — walking down our steep hill to the stores and attending seniors, which was a mile walk. She always made sure that I had a supply of flannel sheets, which she bought at a mall, traveling the five-mile bus ride. Alex, Michele's boyfriend, helps when needed to assist me or to watch mom. Lee, my service dog, gave me assistance, support, love, and confidence. These tasks that I have mentioned are just the tip of the iceberg. I am so fortunate and grateful to have such a loving, dedicated, dynamic support team.

My family has endured my periodic wraths. Early on, I was quick-tempered, frustrated and sometimes a miserable SOB. Over the years, I have become more patient. I must admit, I still get antsy when a tool is used improperly — I'm getting better and still working at it. When I first got home, my mom took me aside and said, "as long as I'm alive, no matter what, I will always take care of you." My mom kept her promise, along with my beloved dad, who never wavered, not once, when it came to my welfare. Out of my parents' six children, I was by far the most rambunctious. When I was injured and in need, none of that mattered to my family. I could not be more blessed in having their love and support. My aspirations always needed a loving hand, and a family member was always there, unconditionally, ready to help fill a void. I am living a beautiful, rewarding life and pursue and accomplish my goals solely because of the love of my wonderful family.

Mom and Dad

Sisters and Brothers

Mom

Dad

Michele and Alex

Brother-in-Law Doug and Mary Ellen

Sister-in-Law Irene and Doug

Brother-in-Law John and Bill

Brother-in-Law Victor and Pat

Grandparents Nanny and Howard

A Wish

After a recent visit to the spinal cord injury clinic, I strolled over to the rehab suite looking for a therapist that I have known for years. I searched, but couldn't locate her. Upon leaving, I saw a young man pushing his gleaming new wheelchair. He looked approximately 20 years old, a recent injury — an assumption on my part. I continued toward the elevator, making my way down to my van. After being loaded up and locked in at my station, I once again saw this young man. This time accompanied by two physical therapists, as they proceeded directly toward a new accessible vehicle. Driving out of the parking structure, we passed what looked like therapists on a tour. Again, another assumption on my part. It all seemed like a synopsis of my last 38 years as a paralyzed man. I recognized myself in this young man, although I had taken similar steps in a longer time frame. I thought about his future. We differed in form of paralysis; me being a mid-level quadriplegic, he a paraplegic. A luxury that we are losing is time. I covet it for a cure — our cure, future cures — which are slipping away much too quickly. I silently wished him a peaceful, fulfilled, happy life.

Grant us the time.

I donate directly all proceeds from the sales of this book to:
The Miami Project to Cure Paralysis

Made in the USA
Coppell, TX
01 August 2023

19825328R00142